Endorsements

"Dr. Ronnie Gaines exemplifies the practical and the spiritual in his personal life. This book does that as well. What a powerful tool it will be to you personally and professionally. Get it. Use it. Grow from it."

—Dr. Jeff Voth
Pastor, Professor, Author of *Cavetime, Defending the Feminine Heart, Why Lewis?* and *A Thousand More Amens*

"Dr. Ronnie Gaines is a specialist in helping couples and congregations grow healthy marriages and restore broken relationships. Dr. Gaines recently led marriage seminars for pastors and their spouses in West Africa through Global Equip resulting in numerous testimonies of personal conviction and life change for these leaders in their own marriages. I am so pleased he has put this wisdom and expertise into the book you now have in your hands. In these pages you will find insight, motivation, and tools for enhancing or resuscitating your marriage. I love the focus of this book on the key issue of being best friends! Dr. Gaines weaves together vital elements for both personal and relational growth enabling marriages to beautifully blossom."

—Dr. John Thompson
Professor of Global Leadership
Founder of Global Equip

BFF

Becoming your spouse's
—— *best friend again* ——

RONNIE GAINES

Published by Freiling Publishing,
a division of Freiling Agency, LLC.

P.O. Box 1264
Warrenton, VA 20188

www.FreilingPublishing.com

PB ISBN: 978-1-956267-32-7
eBook ISBN: 978-1-956267-33-4

Printed in the United States of America

Dedication

TO MY BFF and wife, Mylisa. I am so grateful for you! You have taught me compassion, grace, and patience. I love our Friday date days: hikes, taking trips to see the changing leaves, dinners at the Texas Roadhouse, and driving home listening to 70's music on Pandora. Sometimes we are done eating dinner by 4:30 pm and home before 6:00 pm in our recliners watching a movie; I'm okay with that. Thanks for being my encourager while writing this book and affirming me. I love you, Mis!

To my kiddos, Kimberlynn and Bo. I hope that your mom and I have been good examples of how BFFs are really supposed to be like in a marriage. Thank you for making us proud parents. Do you think I can write a parenting book now?

Also, thank you Daniel for loving and taking care of my daughter (Sweet Cheeks). Thank you both for giving us grandkids; they are truly gifts from God. Bailey, you were the one Bo was searching for all those years. You both are a match! Thank for making him happy.

And, to the greatest joys of a mom and dad; grandkids! Brycen, Gideon, and Gabe, we love you to the moon. You make Mamaw and Popie very happy.

Table of Contents

Introduction

FOR SEVERAL YEARS now, I have had the opportunity and the pleasure to invest many hours into the lives of married couples. Before I even started my master's degree in marital and family therapy, my wife and I met with couples for premarital counseling and those in marriage crisis. One of the reasons I earned my master's degree and followed up with my doctoral degree in the counseling field was to help couples in their marriages. I have a passion to see couples thrive in their relationships, and I believe it is my wheelhouse. At the writing of this book, my wife and I have been married over thirty-three years and we dated for six. We have been together a long time and have experienced just about everything couples are challenged with in a marital relationship. My level of knowledge is not just from my college experience or from my encounters with other couples; I have personal experience. I am great at messing up. I think I create content daily for my credibility to write this book.

My passion began several years go as I saw many couples falling apart in their marriages and giving up;

they were friends of mine. I just couldn't believe that some of them gave up so quickly. Well, to most of us on the outside, it seemed as if they gave up too easily. I know for them it probably seemed like forever arguing and fighting until one of them, or both, just threw in the towel. Even so, I just couldn't imagine giving up something that was once so enjoyable. My wife and I had some rough patches in the past when it came to conflict and arguing, but we always turned it around and worked things out.

My journey became a passion because I wanted to figure out what would cause a couple to end a relationship. The first time he saw her walking down the aisle adorned in that beautiful white wedding gown, he sobbed right in front of his family, his buddies, and the entire audience. She could barely repeat her vows because she was so emotional and overwhelmed by the love she felt for him. They had their first dance as a couple at the reception and looked into each other's eyes as if no one else was in the room. They were truly overwhelmed with a desire with each other unlike anything they had ever felt before. How could it be that after just a few years, they would be sitting in an office with tears of resentment, anger, and failure, not overwhelming love and compassion for each other? They were there to give their relationship one last chance. What causes this to happen so quickly? I became so obsessed to help couples that I got my doctorate with the concentration in the area of helping as many couples save their marriage as I possibly could.

In America today, fifty percent of all marriages fail. Forty-five to fifty percent of first-time marriages and sixty to sixty-three percent of second marriages fail. Seventy percent of third marriages fail, and I can't even imagine the percentages of fourth and fifth marriages. These failures are caused from letting circumstances around us determine the outcome. If these stats are true, and they are, your best chance at marriage is your first. If you are on your second marriage, you have a better chance than with a third, and if this is your third time to be married, it is a better chance compared to a fourth. I am not okay with the data that we have on failed marriages. I know some metrics may be skewed, but for the most part, too many marriages are failing. I want to be part of a solution for recovery and prevention to change the trajectory of this epidemic. You can do this! You can nurture and develop your marriage into a loving, fun-filled, lifetime relationship. Start the process right now. You do not have to be one of the statistics. I want to help you.

When a couple says, *"I do,"* the husband and wife begin a challenging but fulfilling life of laughter, joy, and happiness, and yet it can be filled with many difficulties. Desi Arnaz, the Cuban-born American actor, is best remembered as Ricky Ricardo on the sitcom *I Love Lucy*, launched in 1951. He said, "Good things do not come easy. The road is lined with pitfalls." He is so right! Don't let this discourage you; let it motivate and drive you. Bad things sometimes happen because of complacency and sluggish intentions; however, sometimes they just happen. If we allow the circumstances around us to determine our actions, then when they are not good, we fall apart. But if we do whatever is necessary to make a marriage work, we can defy the incidents that could tear a marriage apart. Change truly does begin in you first, and then things around you will change. Marriage is full of pitfalls. Most of the time, bad relationships are easy to come by, but great relationships take intentionality and work.

If a couple doesn't try, but just lets the "chips fall where they may," a bad relationship can develop much more quickly. I don't believe anyone begins a relationship and says, *"I want this to last a little while and then I want it to 'go south' and fail."* No one wants to have a failed relationship. No one wants a married life of misery and unhappiness. The costs of unsuccessful marriages are so devastating that they do not just affect the couple—they also affect the family and friends. If kids are involved, they feel the pressures and develop personal issues that will follow them their entire lives. When a marriage fails, friends will often be torn between the two sides. Moms and dads suffer from losing a daughter-in-law or son-in-law. The church family experiences hurt as one member moves on due to the failed marriage. It hurts so many.

Your marriage may not seem as passionate as it did in the beginning, but failure is not the end until you quit! It is not over until you end it. Yogi Berra, an American professional baseball catcher and coach said, "It ain't over till it's over." You are just experiencing a circumstance, which can be altered. The result of any circumstance depends on a person's response to it. Steven Covey states, "I am not a product of my circumstances. I am a product of my decisions." Your decisions, not the situation, should determine your outcome. Your decision is the first step in changing anything in your life. Sometimes we look at fear as a bad thing. The fear of losing your lifelong mate might be what causes you to make a decision to change your circumstance.

I have seen couples who say they have tried every method, technique, and approach in an attempt to save their marriage. I have even taught these systematic practices. Most therapists, counselors, and ministers use these tools and methods as well. They usually work, but I have watched couple after couple come back to my office after trying these methods, and they still were falling apart and failing at their relationship. They have even said, *"We have tried everything!"* Everything? Even I started thinking, *"Yes, they have tried everything, and I have, too."*

I would begin by asking, "Name one hundred things that you have tried."

They would say, "Well, maybe not one hundred."

"Name fifty." They couldn't name fifty.

"Name twenty, ten, or five." They couldn't name even five things they tried to change their situation. So I figured out that they had not tried everything.

I kept asking myself, "What is it? What am I doing wrong?" I took it personally. I wanted to know what I was doing wrong that was keeping these couples from finding marital success. I really did think it was my fault and that I needed to find the answer. Then I came to the conclusion that we hadn't tried everything. I dug in and was going to figure this out.

The methods, approaches, and techniques implemented by me, other therapists, counselors, and pastors are basically structural in nature. When a couple starts communicating better, working toward unity, and learning how to deal with conflict in a healthy way, the marriage will become more positive and healthier. I believe these practices are extremely important. However, if a structure is developed first, it may look good for a while, but when storms of contrasting views and strong winds of conflict arise, there is no foundation to hold it together. If you build a house without a foundation but only a structure, as soon as strong winds, torrential rains, and turbulent weather hit, the house will not stand. With a marriage, it may not survive; it could fall apart even while developing and implementing all of these necessary things.

So I began to change the way I did the initial evaluation. I had to find out what was up and why nothing was working. I have always heard that to get the answer that you are looking for, you must ask the right questions. I was asking questions, but I had to start asking the *right* ones. Instead of jumping in to teaching the common techniques, approaches, solutions, and methods that I learned in my academic training, I changed somewhat and would let the spouses interact for a few minutes while I watched and observed. This consisted of body language, how they spoke to each other, their facial expressions while the other was speaking, and how each was influenced by the other—not necessarily whether they were agreeing with each other, but how they reacted when the other was speaking his or her truth.

I watched their level of respect for each other during times of agreement and disagreement. Most of the time, the couples gave me the answer I needed just by listening and watching. My degrees and internship taught me how to implement and teach the usual approaches. But that was not what I was seeing initially. Don't get me wrong—I love these methods, techniques, and approaches. They are the right things to do over an extended period to make a marriage work. That is why so many therapists use them. However, some things must be dealt with before those tools can be effective. I was spending a lot of time going all the way back to the spouses' formative years attempting to figure out the way they viewed marriage as being the major issue. Getting hung up in the past during the initial part of coaching was causing me to miss the vital and necessary aspects of the relationship. It held the sessions captive trying to uncover what the couples' parents did rather than them taking responsibility and saying, *My parents are no longer the problem, and if we are to move forward in our marriage, we must take ownership of our own relationship and build it based on us, not them.*

As I started asking the right questions, the couples begin to tell me what was missing. They didn't just come right out and tell me, but what they were saying to each other through their interactions and behaviors told me what I needed to know to help them start the process to marital success. But don't get the wrong idea here—this is not magic; it is WORK! However, what I discovered was one major aspect that I kept missing all of these years. This would start to change the lives of many couples I would coach. It was a phenomenal developmental advancement for me as a marriage coach. It was so simple that I couldn't believe I had not seen it before. As soon as I saw it, I immediately begin to apply it, and I started seeing a change in couples instantly. What is this BIG secret? It is actually very simple. It is *friendship!*

I saw couples who were in crisis doing everything according to the proverbial marriage counseling book, yet they were still falling apart. But when I begin to add this one piece to the equation, it was a revelational breakthrough. When I began to take a couple through a process of *back in time*—that is, dating—the relationship started to change. Think about this for a moment. If the marriage was great two, three, four, five, or even ten years ago and now it's not, what were you doing back then? What changed?

Right after I had discovered this simple yet profound approach, I was meeting with a husband and wife who were in the middle of a marital crisis. They were hours away from ending their fifteen years together as a married couple. I sat and listened to their story for almost an hour. I watched every move they made, from eye rolls to sighs of disgust. They flailed their arms violently and pointed at each other, justifying their own actions. Each spoke with anger, firing words of mean and disrespectful contempt. A few times, I almost stopped them and made them quit this ill-mannered process, but I just sat back and observed and let them go at it. After several minutes, silence finally brought an end to the hurtful and distasteful rhetoric.

Both individuals looked at me with desperation. They did not even have to say anything to me; I saw it in their eyes. It was a look of *Please help us!* I said, "Can I tell you what I see?" They both nodded. "You both have been doing many things in attempt to help your marriage. You have been to marriage counseling many times. It seems you have tried everything. You are ready to give up. You are tired. You are angry. You want to fix this, but you feel helpless. You're miserable. This is all true, but there is one thing: you both have lost your best friend! He is no longer your best friend. She used to be your best friend, but now you can't stand to be in the room with her. You both are grieving because your best friend no longer exists. He has died! She is gone!"

As soon as these words were out of my mouth, the wife glanced at me, looking as if she had been punched in the stomach. She glared for several moments and then burst into tears. She said, "Yes, that's it! I feel like my best friend is gone. I want my best friend back." By this time, both individuals were weeping. I knew that I had discovered an element that I could always use that would transform couples instantly and get them back on track to creating healthy marriages.

What I discovered was that this couple and others were doing everything right by the book, but they were still falling apart. There was something missing, and this missing piece had to do more with each person individually rather than just doing the right things together. I can't stress enough how important it is to maintain your friendship. I believe it to be so vital that I have written this entire book based on how to revive, nurture, and develop a more meaningful relationship and become your spouse's *Best Friend Forever* (**BFF**) again. I want to give you foundational and structural elements that give stability to a healthy marriage. In the following chapters, you'll learn what couples need to do to develop a master-level marriage and begin to become BFFs all over again. Some of the information may seem strange when you first read it, but you will come to know that it is solid material, and it works.

I hope that you will lean into the content of this book and dream big for your marriage. It is my desire that it will help you develop a strategy that helps you reconnect as a married couple. Work through every chapter as if it is all you have left to live happily ever after. Anything that is worth having takes work, and you can't just hope that everything works out. You cannot just say, "I *hope* our marriage turns around. I *hope* we get our act together and get our marriage back on track." *Hope* is not a strategy. *Intentions* are not strategic. *Intentions* alone are worthless. Knowing what to do is not the power you need for your marital success. In our society today, knowledge is readily available to anyone seeking answers. But it matters what content you choose to absorb; the information you embrace becomes your beliefs, and your beliefs matter when they relate to a healthy marriage. This book is full of solid, well-developed information to bring about good beliefs that you can embrace to help in your marriage. *Knowledge* is not your power but it is your potential power. Putting into practice the ideas in this book *will* change your married life. Action coupled with knowledge is power. Action will transform your marriage.

I have found that anything that you want in life will take some work, and in some cases it will take a huge sacrifice. Your marriage is worth the sacrifice. Your *friendship* is worth every moment you spend in this book. You are worth the sacrifice, and your mate is worth the intense work to create a master-level marriage.

I will take you through a process that will help you gain knowledge, help you apply this knowledge, and help you grow personally and relationally so that ultimately you and your mate will become BFFs all over again. I will teach you foundational and structural application along with tools, methods, and approaches that will ultimately transform your marriage. Some of the information will reinforce what you already know, but much of what I will give you is brand new and innovative. Don't take what you learn from this book lightly; every piece is necessary for the growth of your relationship. I can promise that if you put the instructions into practice, they will transform your relationship.

One thing that I can guarantee is that everything in this book works! I have not only studied and researched this material, but I also live it out. My wife is my BFF, and we build our friendship daily. Do I always do it right? Well, I teach these concepts every day, and I inevitably go home and mess it up. I am just like you; I make mistakes all the time. However, I have learned to recognize when I do things that jeopardize our friendship. When I do, I stop on the spot and say, *"Let me start over; this is not going to work."* Then I do it the right way. I am hardheaded, and sometimes it takes a few minutes before my mind gets on track with what needs to happen and I stop thinking ridiculously. Thank goodness for *"overs."*

I encourage you to take your time through this book and its contents. Start a journal that you can refer to and include page numbers where you can revisit and reiterate concepts and methods of rebuilding your friendship. Sit down as a couple and work through the chapters. Take a chapter each week and discuss the content together. Teach the concepts to your friends. I have learned that if a person reads passively, in four weeks he or she will remember about ten to fifteen percent of what was read. If a person reads and takes notes, in four weeks, fifty to sixty percent of the content will be remembered. However, if one reads, takes notes, and interacts with the content in some form, ninety-plus percent will be remembered after four weeks. This is incredible! Take your time, and make every moment of this book count in your life and marriage.

1

Marriage Blueprint

"Emotionally intelligent couples are intimately familiar with each other's world. I call this having a richly detailed love map."
(John Gottman)

MY DAUGHTER PLAYED high school softball until her senior year along with summer competitive ball. My wife and I went to many games, and we sat in the heat, the cold, the rain, and the misery of many hours of spectating. I can't say we loved every minute, but I would not have missed one moment. We loved that our kids played sports, and I have yelled at many referees for the sake of our team. You know the referee is always wrong, right?

Several years ago, we went to a softball tournament in Oklahoma City, Oklahoma. During those days, we didn't have Google Maps; we had a TomTom GPS. Just like Google Maps, the robotic voice would instruct where to turn, and if the turn was missed, she would tell the driver to reroute, reroute. Oh, how I hated that voice! I don't know what it was about that voice telling me I was wrong. I would talk back to her, and my wife would say, "You realize that she is not real and it doesn't do any good to yell at her." I knew that, but it made me feel better.

The second day, we left the hotel and headed to the same location where we were the day before. I thought I knew exactly where to turn to get to the softball fields. We got to the place that I thought was the correct road, and I turned. Then the voice from "you know where" started saying, "Reroute, reroute." I started the proverbial argument with this woman in a box and continued the route that I had decided was correct and was completely sure the robot was wrong; I actually argued with her.

My wife is the most patient person I know, but she has these looks that are so annoying at times, because I know she is right and I am not going to admit it. She said, "You should have listened!"

But I contended, "This GPS is not right!"

She just said, "You should have listened; this is not the right way."

Now, in my mind I was thinking, *How can she sit there and tell me the right way to go when she doesn't even know north from south?* Her way of giving directions is: "Turn right by the tree that has big green leaves, then go straight until you get to the house with the beautiful flowerbed with pink flowers, then turn left and go maybe two to six more miles, and then the house you are looking for is on the left with really awesome shutters." Really, there are five thousand trees with big green leaves, and is it two miles or six? I will say this, though: if she is driving, she'll take you right to it!

So I was arguing with the GPS and my wife was just sitting there with that look on her face, probably thinking, *If I were driving, we would already be there.* After I realized that I had driven in a complete circle and was at the exact location where I started arguing with the GPS, I said, "Okay, GPS, take me to the field." I went precisely the way she instructed, and I pulled into the softball field parking lot.

Of course, my wife had that smile as if to say, "Yep, I could have told you that!" That was a big lesson for me.

Since this experience, I now listen to the GPS, most of the time. When a plan or destination is entered into the little computer, it will take us to the exact location; it will get us to the place where we want to be. Now, we have GPS apps on our iPhones that will take us on routes that are shorter and faster, and they even let us know when the traffic is backed up. I don't know how we found places without them. I live close to Tulsa, Oklahoma, and we go there quite often. Downtown Tulsa can be confusing if a person is not familiar with the two-way and one-way streets. However, the GPS will maneuver us down the correct roads and take us to the doorstep of our destination.

I would never think about going somewhere I had never been without a plan and a map to get me there. I couldn't even imagine building a structure without a blueprint. You know the neat thing about building a house is that before the house is ever built, someone saw the end result, even before the property was purchased.

In 1994, my wife and I began the task of subcontracting the building of our 2,400-square-foot home. We first met with an architect and gave him a mental picture of what we wanted in our home, and he began to draw every detail. It was amazing how he could see this home in his mind, and when he drew it out, it was exactly what we could see in our minds. The blueprint showed every detail for the contractors who would dig the footing, pour the slab, and structure the house. It gave precise details for the electricians, plumbers, HVAC contractors, sheet rockers, and painters. Every company could see the invisible end result before the finished product was visible. So really, we started with the end in mind first, but it took a blueprint. It took a plan, a map that would help us obtain the finished product that we envisioned.

Do you know where your marriage is going? You may say, "This sounds dumb! We are headed for happily ever after." Great! Is your GPS set for happily ever after? Just because you want to go there doesn't mean that you'll end up there. How do you know where to go? "Well, my mom and dad are there!" If your parents were at a location—let's say Hoot Owl, Oklahoma (which is actually a real town)—and they said, "Come on, join us," you wouldn't just get into your car and drive around. Which way would you go? North? South? East? West? "That's ridiculous! Of course, I have no idea where to go without a map." In the same way, you have no idea where to go in your marriage without a plan; without a map, you will just be driving into the wind with no direction.

Happily ever after is not innate. Do you have a vision for your marriage? Did you create a blueprint for your marriage at the onset? Did you create the plan for your future marital journey? Most couples don't. We may think about how we want it to be and about a blissful life together, but I have seen very few couples who have a plan. Why not draw out a blueprint of your marriage?

We are going to be in this forever. He is going to be your BFF forever. She is going to be your BFF for the rest of your life. Where is your relationship headed? Will you just leave things to chance? Do you have the mindset that *Things will just fall into place on their own*? I believe this is the way most marriages begin; ours did.

This book is all about creating a blueprint for your marriage. It doesn't matter if you have been married one month or twenty years. The fundamentals of becoming BFFs in this book work, no matter how short or how long you have been married.

I was speaking at a marriage conference a few years ago. A couple in the audience had been married for over fifty years. The husband came up to me afterwards and said, "The first night we were here, I thought, what is he going to teach us? We have been married for over fifty years, and I don't want anyone to mess this up. Everything is fine." He went on to tell me, "But after the first night, I understood that even after fifty years of marriage, this was some good stuff. I can do this and make our marriage better." I can't count the times when a husband and wife would tell me that their marriage was so good that nothing could make it better, but when they heard these fundamentals that you will discover in these pages, they were able to create a better BFF relationship with each other.

Make a plan for your future. Create a blueprint of what you need to do to make your relationship a master-level marriage. To do this, you must change your beliefs about marriage. It's one thing to have a desire to have a great marriage, but it's much more to go beyond desire and actually implement strategies to create it. Past embedded ideologies of what marriage is supposed to be are not creating your blueprint. You may say, "My parents' marriage was good, and mine will be good as well." They may have had a great marriage, but your dad is not your husband, and your mom is not you. You are completely different individuals, and you have different dynamics in your relationship than your parents. On the flip side of this, maybe your parents had a miserable marriage and it is not a good model at all.

It matters what you believe about how your marriage should be. You need to give some attention to your past experience about marriage. This is not to contradict what I wrote in the introduction, but coming to terms with what you have been taught or experienced in the past will give you an idea of why you believe the way you do about the relationship with your spouse. Your beliefs will determine how you see your marriage. Your beliefs will define how you think about a BFF relationship with your spouse. Your beliefs will direct the decisions you make for your marriage. Your beliefs about marriage will determine your marriage blueprint. How you believe about a certain conflict will determine the outcome. How you believe shapes your decisions and your actions, and a lot of your beliefs are embedded from your formative years. However, some of these beliefs must change to create the blueprint for your marriage. Whatever you draw out or paint for your marriage will become its identity, and some of the past ideologies have to go.

You may have had a horrible example of marriage growing up. However, blaming your parents must come to an end if you want to progress in a healthy marriage with your mate. It's up to you now to discover and design your blueprint for a successful marriage. Quit the blame game and develop your blueprint. You are not entitled to a great marriage; you must create it and believe that you can do so. Believe that when you implement these strategies, you will be on your way to marital success. Believe your marriage can be different from your past examples. Believe that the two of you have everything you need to become *your* version of the relationship for you.

You may think that a messed-up blueprint of your marriage is a way to end up in a marital disaster. Some may even believe that not having a blueprint at all would be just as devastating. But there is no such thing as not having a blueprint. Your blueprint began during your formative years. Without even thinking about it, you were developing a cognitive blueprint of marriage at a young age; it was automatic. Now you must erase your former idea and replace it with your new impression of marriage. You may say, "I had a really great example of marriage growing up." Fine, but don't rely on that too much. Yes, there are things you can glean from, and your parents can help you tremendously. But you must create your own blueprint based on you and your mate.

We spend a lot of time planning for many other things in our lives: mapped-out trips, grocery lists, weekly meal plans, intense workouts, Christmas shopping, speeches, dream home plans, and even wedding plans, yet most couples never create a blueprint for marriage. Maybe we have been programmed to believe that once a couple says, "I do," things just fall into place. I wish it were that easy. This sort of thinking is why so many couples are struggling in their marriages today. They are shocked that their relationships are in such a mess. "What happened?

I thought..." Is the dream over? I am here to tell you that it doesn't have to be over. It is time to regroup, start a plan, and create a blueprint. Not just any blueprint, but the *right* blueprint. Picture the landscape of what you want your marriage to look like. Create a detailed blueprint to give direction to your future. Here are a few ways to create your marriage blueprint.

Create Expectations

Do you know what your mate expects from you in the marriage? *"Sure, I am supposed to be his wife!"* What does that even mean? *"She wants me to be the man of the house."* Can you define that? I love this segment in coaching sessions, especially in premarital counseling. It's so much fun compared to a marriage in crisis. It is pleasant, and both individuals are so much in love. *"He has the most wonderful parents; I just love them both."* *"She is so perfect, and her family is so awesome!"* I seriously laugh every time I hear couples say things like this. I'm not making light of it; it is just funny. They really do believe it at this point. But things sure change after a short time. *"I wish his mom would stay out of our business!"* *"Her dad thinks I am an idiot and that I don't know how to take care of my own house."* This is what often happens after the initial premarital sessions. This is why I love the expectation sessions because I create tension. Why would I want to create tension in a premarital session? I would rather the couple experience this tension before the wedding than to experience it sometime after the ceremony without a mediator.

In the expectation sessions, I ask the future husband and wife to create a list of at least ten expectations they have for each other and bring it to one of the sessions. This list must be behaviorally specific and something that the other can do personally. Oh, the items that surface on these lists. I have seen couples go from the ooey-gooey, lovey-dovey emotions to an instant, "You're kidding!" I have heard things like: *"I expect her to always work out and be thin"*; *"I expect him to always have a job"*; *"I expect him to always be the leader in the home and make sure everyone in the house gets up and goes to church"*; *"I expect her to never be controlling and nagging"*; *"I expect us to have only two kids"* (this is a big contrasting one at times); and *"I expect her to learn how and do all of the cooking."* These are just a few, and I have found that this exercise helps face the elephant in the room that could cause a major blow-up later in the relationship. It allows the truth of each person's expectations to surface early so that the couple can deal with it sooner rather than later.

This is not something I do just for premarital counseling; I do this in all of my sessions. It is much easier to implement in a premarital context, but it is necessary for any stage of the relationship. I encourage you to sit down with each other and discuss your expectations. Sometimes it is unsaid expectations that are not being met that are causing many problems. We complain and we get frustrated, angry, and hurt because expectations have not been met, and all along, they have never been communicated. The lack of communication causes frustration and resentment.

What really makes a quality marriage? Loving her unconditionally? Respecting him unconditionally? Picking up your clothes throughout the house without being asked? Having his favorite meal cooked when he gets home from work? Ensuring that her car is full of fuel? All of these things are necessary and good, but the quality of your marriage is a matter of meeting each other's expectations. Being intentional about expectations brings us to a place of better communication and speaking our truth in love.

I am the pastor of one of the greatest churches in Oklahoma. Yes, I am a little biased. However, over the years, I have put several people into leadership positions. Everything would go well for a while and then, seemingly out of the blue, a leader would stop doing what he or she should be doing for that position—or what *I* expected should be done. I would get extremely frustrated, and I wanted to replace the person immediately. I wanted to get someone else in there who would *do it right*. "This person should know what to do! I can't believe the leader will not carry out what needs to be done in this position!" Then, with some help from my wife, who is really good at calming me and helping me see reality, I began to realize that I had never communicated my expectations of the position. The person thought the job was being done well. I thought it was the worst. My expectations were different from what the leader thought was expected. It wasn't that the person was doing anything that was poor quality; it just wasn't what I wanted. It wasn't what I expected. Soon, I implemented systems and blueprints of what was expected, and we wrote out what needed to be done. This was a breakthrough in our church leadership.

It is not fair to your relationship to *not* communicate your expectations. However, you do need to know what you expect; this is part of your marital blueprint. What do you do if your mate does not agree with your expectations and refuses to comply? Well, this is more of a complicated dynamic if a couple is already married versus dating. If you are dating and the expectation is a huge conviction, you may need to reconsider the continuation of the relationship. *"Oh, I could never do that; we are too far into this. I love him."* Listen to me closely. If this matter is not settled and expectations are not brought into alignment, there will be major problems down the line. You must take care of it now. *"What if we are already married and we discover there is a discrepancy in our expectations and neither of us wants to budge? Do we just end the marriage?"* That's a ridiculous thought. No, you don't just end the marriage; however, both of you must communicate your truths and come to an agreement. It might mean that one of you must accept the other's idea. There is a difference between acceptance and approval. You may have to accept it, and it could be a thorn in your side for the rest of your marriage. You will have to understand and accept your decisions.

Before one of you, out of the blue, begins asking or communicating expectations, discuss this portion of the book together and talk about hearing each other's thoughts. Maybe after a discussion, each one of you could go off on your own and list ten expectations and come back together and discuss them. I recommend not only having expectations, but also providing reasons why you believe the way you do. I have found that leading with the *why* is so much more productive, and it adds a softer approach to what is expected. Just remember, unmet expectations can lead to an unhealthy relationship, so do this as soon as possible.

Another thing about expectations is to be reasonable. Once I met with a husband and wife and had them do the expectations exercise. The husband mentioned that he was extremely upset because of his wife's sister who criticized him all the time. He expected his wife to stop it. But it was out of her power to make her sister do anything, or in this case, to make her stop doing it. She had no control over her sister. In fact, the sister was so arrogant that she listened to no one. There was no stopping her. This was something that his wife was not capable of doing, so I suggested that they set boundaries with the sister, especially his wife, and allow the sister to have dealings with them only under strict rules. If she couldn't abide by the rules, the wife should protect her relationship with her husband and put some distance between them and the sister.

I have had couples in my office where the husband expected his wife to have sex with him anytime he wanted, but this is not reasonable. I get it, men—you may have thought when you were young, *When I get married, I will be able to have sex anytime I want it*. If you have been married just a few weeks (or seconds), you'll realize how foolish that sounds. The expectations exercise is to be reasonable and doable by both individuals. Stop here before you proceed and complete your expectations list.

Create a Financial Plan

I won't write a lot about the financial aspects of marriage here, but this is a major part of developing a marriage blueprint. There are many books and programs available that can help you set up a financial plan. I believe the best plan for beginners or for those in a lot of debt is the Ramsey Solution plan. You can find everything you need for this at www.ramseysolutions.com. However, I will touch on a couple of things that I believe are important. First, I believe both of you should have a grasp on where you are financially and the debt you have accrued. One of you may have the primary responsibility of paying the bills and taking care of the finances, but neither should be in the dark concerning the finances in the household. Both of you should be in the know.

Your plan and method may be different from your parents, friends, or anyone you know, but agree on the approach. When my wife and I were first married, we didn't have debit cards. At that time, we didn't even have credit cards; we used checks. We started out with one account. I believe that *What's mine is mine and what's hers is mine.* Just kidding! There were times when I would be out fishing and I had taken the checkbook out of her purse. While I was gone, she went to the grocery store, walked up to the front to check out, and realized that she did not have the checkbook. She wasn't happy that she had to leave the full basket of groceries and go home. After this happened a couple of times, things changed. We opened another account with both of our names on it, and we called this one *her account.* We both had access, but it was used for some things while my account was used for all other purchases or bills.

This may not be your way, but it worked for us. It was our blueprint. She knew what went in and out of my account, and I knew what went in and out of her account. It worked out great. The idea is not to copy someone else but to have a blueprint of what works for you, even when it comes to planning your investments, savings, expenditures, big vacations, and retirement. Create a financial blueprint early and then alter the plan throughout the years.

Discuss and Plan Life Dreams

One element that will stall or put a halt to a marriage is when the couple stops dreaming. I have heard couples say, "Dreaming just causes problems in our marriage because it distorts reality." How sad. What would it be like to live life and never dream? Using our imagination is one of the greatest qualities that set us apart from every other creature, and dreaming has brought about some phenomenal inventions.

In 1919, Walt Disney was fired from the *Kansas City Star* for lacking imagination and creativity, but he was a dreamer. He dreamed bigger than any one job. Later, he had to file for bankruptcy due to the failure of his animated studio idea called Laugh-o-Gram. But Walt never stopped dreaming. In 2020, the Walt Disney Company's total income was over $8 billion. What if he had allowed other people's opinions stop his ability to dream?

I read an article in which a reporter was interviewing Walt's brother and stated how sad it was that Walt never got to see the finished Disney World. His brother looked at the reporter and said, "This is why you'll never be anything more than a reporter." He went on to say, "Walt did see it finished; he saw it before the breaking of the ground." We must see the end before the beginning.

Dream big for your marriage. See it being incredible, fascinating, enjoyable, and fulfilling. See yourself being everything *you* can be. See your marriage five years from now. Ten years. Twenty years. What do you want to accomplish in your relationship fifty years from now? What is your *dream* vacation? What is your dream for your finances in five, ten, fifty years? Never stop dreaming. Create a dream blueprint for your marriage.

Discuss Plans for Children

How many kids do you want? As mentioned above, this is an important question or expectation for married couples. "We'll just have how ever many God wants us to have." I realize that some believe that this is how God intended it, while others take precautions and attempt to control the number of children they have. Here is the thing: whichever way you believe, it's good if the two of you are on the same page. Discuss this with each other and communicate your expectations. Create your blueprint for having kids. I get it, there may be an *oops* that you weren't expecting; these things can happen. My wife and I have two children; our daughter is twenty-nine and our son is twenty-eight. They are eighteen months apart. Now, eighteen months was not planned; there was an *oops*. However, we had a blueprint of two years apart, so it was close.

In contrast to what I teach now, my wife and I never discussed our expectations of how many kids we wanted. I really don't remember ever thinking or talking about a particular number. After having our son, my wife developed some medical issues, and her doctor indicated that if we were going to have any more children, we needed to do it immediately because my wife needed to have a complete hysterectomy. We discussed it. Well, I think the discussion was more like this: I was saying, "I'm done." I thought two was plenty. The biggest highlight for me was when my kids could poop and wipe themselves. Instead of hearing, "I'm done!" which means, *Come and wipe me,* they just went on their own. I didn't want to go through all of that again. The potty training was over, and I was celebrating.

One day the kids were with me and my wife was working. We were in the process of potty training my son. My wife had purchased some training underwear for him. I was on duty (I should say that I was really on doody watch). My son did not tell me he needed to go so, he did the #2 in these so-called training pants. It was not good. I took them off of him and threw them in the trash. My mistake was that I didn't hide it. When my wife got home, she found the soiled pants. She took them out and cleaned them, and I got the explanation of how they are to be cleaned and not thrown out. My response was: "If I can go to Walmart and get a package of three for five bucks, I am not going to do the washy-washy thing in the stool; the pants are going in the trash!" After getting past this, I just couldn't see going through the whole thing again with another child.

The main thing is that we discussed it and came to an agreement to not have any more kids. It wasn't her decision, but I believe she compromised by acceptance, not agreement; she really did want more kids. But here is the deal: God has blessed her with three grandkids so far, and she is a happy Mamaw.

Discuss and Plan Retirement

A lot of resources are out there to help with the subject of retirement, so I am going to make this really short. Plan your retirement! There will come a day when you *will* retire, either by force or by choice. Your beliefs and decisions now will drastically influence how your future retirement will look. Will it be golden, or will it be iron-clad devastating? You may be young now, but time keeps ticking. It seems like yesterday that my wife and I were in our twenties and we weren't discussing our retirement plans. If we had done so, we would have been further along toward our goals. But we are still on a trajectory to land in retirement well; however, if we hadn't visited this sometime back, it would not look so good right now. Our blueprint is set, and we are intense. Learn from me: plan your retirement and agree on the blueprint necessary to meet your goals.

These are just a few things that will help you create your blueprint for your marriage. "If you fail to plan, you plan to fail." This is true in marriage as well. Your marital blueprint is very important. Don't leave it undone. Sit down together now and create a destination for your marriage. Create a blueprint and start building.

2

Change the Way You Think

"That which dominates our imagination and our thoughts
will determine our lives, and our character."
(Ralph Waldo Emerson)

IN THE 1967 classic movie *Cool Hand Luke*, Paul
Newman stars as Luke Jackson. Luke is a cool, gutsy
prisoner in a Southern chain gang due to his crime of
destroying parking meters.

One evening, Luke Jackson got extremely drunk and
begin cutting down parking meters with a large pipe
cutter. This offense landed him in prison. While refusing
to buckle under the authority of the warden and the
prison guard officials, he kept trying to escape without
success. All the other prisoners admired Luke, but the
prison staff actively worked to crush Luke's spirit until
he finally broke.

This movie had many one-liners that people still use
to this day. *"What we have here is a failure to communicate"* was one of the most popular lines. However,

one classic line was spoken by the warden after Luke had escaped and was recaptured. As the guards dragged him into the living quarters with all prisoners looking on, they flung the half-beaten, non-responsive, lethargic Luke Jackson to the floor in the middle of the room. The warden spoke: *"You run one time, you got yourself a set of chains. You run twice, you got yourself two sets. You ain't gonna need no third set 'cause you gonna get your mind right."*

If there is one huge factor that will ultimately transform your marriage, this is it: "You gotta get your mind right!" In fact, this process will transform anything in your life: how you interact at work, the way you relate with your kids, how you handle your money and finances, and how you mature spiritually. It will also help you in personal development and advance you into becoming your best self.

This concept is not new. Many books and resources are available concerning this topic. It will help you become who you really want to be. It will help you create your future best self. If you can grasp this concept and put it into daily practice, your life will never be the same. You will begin to build wealth and have a better relationship with your kids, your extended family, and your co-workers. Your marriage will thrive, not just survive. You will ultimately create a master-level marriage. What is it? It's what the warden said in the movie *Cool Hand Luke*: "*You gonna get your mind right.*" The key to everything, and I mean everything in life, is to get your mind right.

I have come to the conclusion that if a person can change the way he or she thinks about anything, it **will** change the outcome. Andy Stanley, pastor of North Point Community Church in Atlanta, Georgia, in his book *The Principle of the Path: How to Get from Where You Are to Where You Want to Be*, states: "Direction, not intention, determines destination." What we set our minds to will determine our behavior and the outcome for our destiny. At the writing of this book, I have been working toward getting certified as a life and health and wellness coach. One thing that I have learned is that everything we do and become has to do with three elements: beliefs, behaviors, and identity.

Beliefs

I have been teaching this process for quite some time. It really does matter how and what you believe. Your voice is the most influential voice in your head. You will believe and do whatever you tell yourself. Although your beliefs are partly from the way you were raised and are influenced by your embedded family of origin, it still comes down to what you tell yourself. When you believe in something strong enough, no one will be able to change your mind.

Recently our country faced the challenge of putting a new president into office. Some voters believed that Joe Biden was the answer to turning our country around, and you could not convince them otherwise. Their beliefs were set, and they truly believed it. On the other hand, some felt that if President Donald Trump did not resume office, the country would surely go under. That was their belief, and no one could change their minds. The only way they could do so is to change their minds themselves. No one could do it for them. Someone might give some compelling ideas and information that would cause the change, but it is ultimately an individual decision.

In the next few pages, I intend to encourage you to think differently about how you think. From this point until the end of this chapter, I will put aside any marital approaches and concepts as the central topic and focus on the mind. If we can't get this right, no tools or methods will work properly. My purpose is to get you to practice thinking differently and learn to view things in a different light so that you could possibly change your mind.

I love the old black-and-white *The Andy Griffith Show* from the 1960s. I have probably watched every episode a thousand times. In one particular episode, Gomer Pyle decides to join the Marine Corps. Andy, the sheriff, does his best to talk him out of it. Gomer is a simple country boy who is extremely naïve about anything to do with life; he doesn't have a lot of common sense. In spite of Andy's attempts in talking him out of it, Gomer is determined to become a marine.

Andy takes Gomer to boot camp, and in his first few minutes in formation, he becomes senior drill instructor Sergeant Carter's thorn in the flesh. From that point on, Gomer was always in trouble with the sergeant. One time after Gomer really messed up, Sergeant Carter had him stand by his bunk with a bucket over his head and told him to stand there and think about what he had done. On one of Andy's many visits to check on Gomer, Andy snuck up to the barracks window and found Gomer standing there with the bucket over his head. He got Gomer's attention and questioned him about it in a whisper. Gomer, so glad to see Andy, said, *"The sergeant said that I should put this bucket over my head and thank."* Andy inquired, *"What are you thinking about?"* Gomer replied, *"I was just thanking how easy it was to stand here and thank!"*

Sometimes, I believe we need to put a metaphorical bucket over our heads and just think about how easy it is to think or change the way we think. In other words, we must change the way we think about how we think.

Many marriage coaches, counselors, and therapists are ready to help couples transform their marriages. The cost will range anywhere from $40 to $175 per session. In some cases, marriage coaches and counselors are charging as much as $400 to $600 for a two-hour session. The difference in these professionals is the price. The comparison is that the majority of them will teach the same techniques, skills, tools, and methods. Unfortunately, the tools will not magically transform your marriage; however, the way you think about your marriage will.

I love to jog. Some of you are like my wife: "The only time you will see me running is if something is chasing me." I get it! Jogging is not for everyone, but I love getting out on the asphalt and just taking off. When I was growing up, I never jogged. I didn't even know that

I loved it or was good at it until I started training to join the Marine Corps. Now, thirty-five years later, I'm still jogging—not quite as fast, but nonetheless, I still love to run. I put in a good number of miles each week.

Just this morning, I got up early, consumed the right amount of water and carbohydrates for energy, and dressed appropriately for the 25-degree weather. I love jogging in cold temperatures. In fact, when I hit the pavement, I thought to myself, *This is awesome!* I usually listen to a podcast, an audio book, or something related to some sort of teaching or personal development when I run. I always have a distance goal in mind—usually three to six miles on a normal run day. I have always set a certain distance to complete on every run unless it is a race such as a 5K, 10K, or a half-marathon. Once I reach the preset distance, sometimes I keep going and push myself. But I nearly always complete what I set my mind to. Sometimes I feel as if I'm running out of energy and start thinking, *I'm not going to make my goal.* However, there have been very few times when I was not able to finish.

I have learned that when I feel as if I am not going to make it, I set my mind to think differently. I might even focus my mind on something other than jogging. I'll start listening more intently to the podcast and get my mind focused on learning something instead of thinking about how I feel. I have learned to get my mind right.

When a thought enters the mind, several things happen in just a few milliseconds. Once you receive certain information, the brain will generate an interpretation of the content. As soon as an interpretation is given, a feeling connects to that interpretation. Your brain moves from the logical to the affective. Feelings then promote behaviors, and the behaviors lead to an effect or consequence. The interpretation stage is the critical one.

Zig Zigler says, "If you want your life to change, watch what comes into your mind." This is true, but what about those thoughts that make it in? We are not superhuman, and sometimes thoughts don't get cast down before entering. It is so difficult to say to yourself every time, *"Nope, you can't get in there!"* or *"Oh no, there comes that thought again; shut the door!"* So what do you do when certain thoughts do get in? You must be intentional about what you do with them. You need to keep out every bad thought that you can, and it matters what you do with those that do get in. One writer in the ancient text states, "Cast down those thoughts." In other words, when bad thoughts come in, check them out and cast them down. Let's look at the stages of how our mind works.

Information

The brain is extremely scientific and more complicated than I can explain within the scope of this book, but I want to create a foundation to show what happens with our thoughts and what we need to do with them. Information fills our minds every moment of every day. Whatever the information is, it goes to the storage area where it remains until we do something with it. An area located in the inner part of our brain called the hippocampus is associated primarily with memory. Research shows that the hippocampus receives the information from neurotransmitters such as serotonin, norepinephrine, and dopamine, and then it distributes it to the rest of the brain. Some studies indicate that it stores memory for a long term and makes these memories resistant to forgetting. This can be great for those things that are necessary to remember. When we get good quality sleep, that is, through every stage of sleep throughout the night, our short-term memory gets converted to long-term memory. More on this later.

At this stage, these are just thoughts. It could be something that you saw on TV or that you read in a book or on the web. It could be something that was said to you at work or that your spouse said or did. Still, it is just information at this level. These thoughts can be negative, positive, unimportant, or so important that you need to remember them or something bad could happen. Whatever the reason, after receiving the information, you will interpret it.

Interpretation

Every piece of information that comes into the brain is interpreted in some way. If you scroll across a post on Facebook and the first sentence does not capture your interest, you interpret it as unimportant and will keep scrolling. Maybe one of the posts that you see is from one of your friends who is always posting selfies taken via the bathroom mirror, and you think none of those pictures should be on any social media outlet. You then take this information and interpret it as, *She is so dramatic!* Interpretation is all about constructing my belief about what the information means to me. These are my thoughts and opinions, not necessarily facts.

Once information has been interpreted, what follows is the next stage: feelings.

Feelings

Once information is interpreted, it transfers to the affective part of our brain; feelings follow interpretation. *The information is boring, so I don't care; I'll keep scrolling. She always posts the most ridiculous pictures, so I feel annoyed.* By now, if you are following the pattern of these stages, you are probably starting to realize how this relates to your marriage and how you and your mate receive information, how you interpret it, and how it makes you feel. *He ate his dinner and never said a word the entire time. He drank the last drop of his tea, burped, and then got up and went to his recliner. He never said anything about whether dinner was good or bad* (**information**). *He didn't like it* (**interpretation**). *I feel hurt* (**feelings**). Remember, thoughts are opinions; they're not facts. She is not sure if that is really what he was thinking. In fact, this may not even enter his mind, but it is her interpretation, and it causes the hurtful feelings. This is how our brains work. After receiving the information, interpreting the content, and experiencing the feelings connected to our own attribution, it will initiate the next step: a behavior.

Behavior

For every feeling, there is a behavior. A response follows a feeling. I feel hurt, I cry. I feel angry, I throw something. I feel fear, I run! I feel appreciated, I smile. Using the examples from the previous stage; I read the Facebook post (**information**). It is boring (**interpretation**). I don't really care (**feelings**). I keep scrolling (**behavior**). In the second example, he ate his dinner and never said a word the entire time (**information**). Then he drank the last drop of his tea, burped, got up, and went to his recliner. He never said anything about dinner. He didn't like it (**interpretation**), and that hurts my feelings (**feelings**). She goes to the other room and cries (**behavior**). After a behavior comes the **effect** (consequence).

Effect

Effects (consequences) follow feelings. "My feelings were hurt because he didn't say anything about dinner" (**she is crying**). "See if I work that hard cooking for him again!" The evening ends with silence and frustration (**effect**).

Let's alter the scene. He comes home from work, walks through the door, sits down to eat, never says anything about the meal, gets up, and makes his way to his recliner. She interprets this as something must be wrong. He was okay when he left this morning, and we haven't seen each other all day, so something happened between this morning and now.

She approaches him and asks, "Is everything okay?"

He responds, "I'm sorry! I had a lot on my plate today at work, and I just have a lot on my mind with everything to do with my job."

Most of the time in marriage, when something is not quite right, it has little to do with the internal and more to do with the external. Notice how changing the interpretation changes everything. Most of the time, we interpret the information wrongly. The best way to know how to interpret information is by asking—this will change everything.

It matters what you do with the information that comes into your mind. Even people with a winning mentality, even those who possess a master-level attitude, are at times bombarded by negative or destructive thoughts. However, master-level individuals create self-talk that transforms their cognitive functions. Your voice is truly the most influential voice in your life. You will do whatever you tell yourself. The mind is unique, and self-talk is one of the greatest tools you have to produce whatever outcome you desire.

Now, back to my jogging story. A few weeks ago, on another one of my runs, I tried a new technique to see what my mind would do. There is usually a time when I start to feel my body tiring, I finish my goal distance, and then I'm done. But on this particular day, I wanted to see how far I could go, even if I felt fatigue. What would happen if I re-programmed my mind, no matter how my body felt? I wanted to see if the old adage, *mind over matter*, was correct. What would happen if I changed the way I thought? So I set my goal and started running.

As soon as I completed the pre-determined distance, I decided to let my body choose if it wanted to stop at my goal or continue. When I turned it over to my body, it said, "I'm done!" But when I let my body decide, it told me that it was tired and sluggish and it wanted to quit, but my mind was saying to me, "Come on, you can go another quarter of a mile. No, go another half a mile. Come on, you can keep going." Needless to say, I

continued even though I was feeling exhausted and sluggish. I completed another mile before stopping. I discovered that even though I let my body have a say, I still
changed the way I thought about the situation. I found
out that it is truly "mind over matter."

My mind had the **information,** and the **interpretation** was that my body was tired, and I could *feel* the
exhaustion. However, this is the critical point of any
information that enters the mind. Here is where I determined what I would do with the information. It mattered
how I interpreted the stimulus that was presented.
Remember, a behavior always follows a feeling, and if
we change how we interpret the information received,
it will alter our feeling and the behavior will change the
outcome. When I became exhausted and thought I was
done, my mind changed and altered the information,
which allowed me to run an additional mile. The *effect*
was a longer period of an elevated heart rate and more
calories burned. BOOM!

When you learn how to change the way you think,
it will transform your marriage. Whatever you give
attention to will determine your outcome. Just as Andy
Stanley stated, it is truly direction, not intention, that
determines your outcome. *My intention is to start the*

conversation with my wife using a soft approach. In reality, *The more I thought about her nasty tone* (**information/ interpretation**), *the more it ticked me off* (**feeling**). The more you give attention to what she said, the more you get frustrated. Now, you blow up and you vent on her (**behavior**). Your intentions were to start with a soft approach, but you gave more attention to what she said rather than how to approach it softly (you wanted to change the way you thought, but instead, you relapsed to the original **interpretation/feeling**). Now, you lose it (**undesired behavior**). **Effect:** you're sleeping in the doghouse, my friend!

Practice today on some little things. Take a less intense moment when the information is presented and practice changing how you perceive it. You have heard the saying, "Practice makes perfect." Well, that is not true. Practice does not make perfect; practice makes permanent. Practice the wrong things in your relationship, and you will get bad results. Practice good things, and you get good life-long results.

Behaviors

The second thing that I learned from my certification is that whatever we believe, our behaviors follow. If I believe that I can't accomplish something, there is a good possibility that I will never behave in a way to accomplish it. In fact, if my beliefs are in contrast to a certain reality, my behaviors will be in contrast as well. When I believe that it doesn't do any good for my health to cut back on simple carbohydrates (sugary foods), I will continue to consume donuts, cookies, cake, etc., and pack on fat as those carbs turn to sugar and store up in my fat cells. However, if I research, study, and understand what these carbs actually do to my body, I begin to interpret things differently and alter the way I think about them. Once I believe differently, my behavior begins to follow my beliefs.

It is the same with spirituality. As a Christian, I believe in the old ancient book, the Bible. I don't just believe parts of it and discard the rest. I chose years ago to embrace every part of it. I don't understand everything about the content, but I have determined to believe in Scripture, whether I completely understand it or not. By faith, I choose to follow, to the best of my ability, the path of the passages. Many times I fail, and I have to readjust to get back on track. However, because of my belief in the authenticity of the Scriptures, my behaviors align with the written words of the authors.

When a person believes a certain way, behaviors will be a byproduct of those beliefs. *"He did that on purpose!"* This belief will determine how a wife behaves when her husband walks into the room. He comes home and negative confrontation is inevitable. *"How dare you do this to me? You are so inconsiderate!"* Now, notice this completely different scenario: *"I'm not sure if he did that on purpose, but I'm hurt, and I want to discuss his intentions."* He comes home, and she confronts him with the complaint rather than criticism. If the belief is different, the behavior will be different, and so will the outcome.

Change your belief, change your life! Change the way you believe about certain circumstances in your relationship and change the trajectory of your marriage. Believe your way to a great marriage.

Identity

Identity is how you and others see you. Behaviors will determine your relationship identity. This is the third thing I learned from my certification. A person will become how he or she believes and acts, and a relationship will become how each person believes and behaves. Behavior cannot be separated from beliefs, and identity cannot be separated from behaviors. A person can want his or her identity to be seen one way, but behaviors determine the identity. The Bible calls these behaviors fruits. The Good Teacher said, "A good tree produces good fruit, and a bad tree produces bad fruit. A good tree can't produce bad fruit, and a bad tree can't produce good fruit. So, every tree that does not produce good fruit is chopped down and thrown into the fire. Yes, just as you can identify a tree by its fruit, so you can identify people by their actions." So how you behave determines your identity.

I have seen many individuals who were raised in households of screaming, chaotic parents. The parents created a home where there was only one way to handle conflict: they just screamed and yelled. Some might call it dysfunctional. However, this was all that these families knew. They just yelled and screamed, and the whole household was disrupted. They called it communicating. I see these same kids who are now grown and have their own family systems, and the environment is yelling and screaming. The legacy of a screaming and yelling identity continues. The only way for them to change their identity is to alter their beliefs about conflict and how the family system should function, and this will change their behaviors. A new identity will be created. If you want your marriage to be a certain way or want to change your marital system, you must have a picture of your future relationship—begin seeing this new picture. The new landscape will govern your beliefs, and your beliefs will produce good behaviors, which will result in your new identity as a couple.

The success, longevity, and wholesome and healthy outcome of your marital relationship will truly manifest by the way you think. The process of changing the way you think is not just on a personal level, but it also matters how you think collectively. Couples must work on coming into agreement on matters of the relationship. I don't believe that collectively coming to an agreement means that a person loses his or her independence. Sometimes we just don't get our own way! If both of you have completely different opinions on a matter, changing the way you think doesn't mean giving up your autonomy. It doesn't mean being passive and giving in and losing.

There are some battles (conflicts) that are not the hill you should try to win. Compromise doesn't mean that you lost; it means that this was necessary for today. Think differently about why you want to win or be right. Is it because you are right, or is it because you want to win and be right at all cost? I like to say it like this: There is her truth, his truth, and the real truth. Sometimes to find the real truth, both individuals must put aside their thoughts, feelings, and wants and search for resolution. This takes changing the way you think. For now, put aside every part of your desire to be right and win. Change the way you think, and focus and strive for resolution through compromise. You can either seek to compromise and work toward unity or spend your entire marriage living in chaos until "death do us part" or until you throw up your hands and quit early.

You can do this! I don't believe you entered into this marital relationship to end up with a lack of understanding, lack of commitment, lack of good communication, lack of compromise, and lack of mutual resolution. I believe you started your marriage to enjoy being with someone you love and to ultimately spend the rest of your life at peace and harmony. However, for this to happen, you must change your way of thinking about certain situations while not presupposing. This will allow you to avoid contaminating your relationship before knowing the facts. Create the marital identity that you want!

3

We're in Love!

*"If you have fallen out of love with your mate,
go back and court like you did when you first fell in love,
and you will fall back in love."*
(Zig Zigler)

I KNOW A couple who never dated much; they were both very picky. Both were gifted in looks. She is beautiful, spends a lot of time at the gym, has the most up-to-date and stylish clothes, has perfect makeup, and is very fit. She is very attractive. He is slender and fit and works out at the gym every day. He has good teeth, nice hair, and gets a lot of looks from the girls. However, through the years, neither dated very many people. They both had this idea that it was a waste of time to keep a relationship going that would never lead to marriage. Why date a person who was not marriage material? So they waited and searched, and then they found each other. They both like being fit, they love hiking and biking, and they are both coffee snobs. By the way, if I walk into a coffee shop and ask for a *pour-over* and they give me a confused look, I go somewhere else. I'm kind of a coffee snob as well. Sorry, back to the story.

When they met for the first time, in a coffee shop, he thought, *"This is the one."* They never dated anyone else again and married just before they celebrated their second first-date anniversary. The initial love experience had infected them. Not all relationships have this type of story. In fact, first dates often end as soon as they start. She realizes that he is not what she expected. He is weird. The journey ends, and the initial love experience never begins. However, there are those who go out for a second date and then a third, fourth, fifth, and so on, and then, BAM! the feeling hits them.

This feeling or experience causes lack of sleep, missed meals, and many conversations on the phone for hours not really saying anything: *"You hang up!" "No, you hang up!" "No. I'll hang up when you hang up."* Oh, just hang up already. It generates late-night texting and a lot of money spent.

My wife and I were no different, even thirty-eight years ago. It seems annoying now, but when couples experience this feeling, they do stupid and ridiculous things. I joined the Marine Corps when I was twenty-one, and I was dating my wife during that time. We were over two thousand miles away from each other and communicated by payphone. For you younger readers, a payphone was in a glass booth, and you would insert money into the phone to make your call. Or you could use a credit card to pay for it. We found ways to use codes that would allow is to talk for hours, and it never cost us a thing. Yes, it was illegal, but I didn't care back then; I was getting to talk to the love of my life for FREE! But I know somebody was paying for it. I can't imagine getting those bills in the mail from all of the Marines who used those codes. When someone caught on to the huge bills, the code would not work, but somebody always had another one.

My wife and I would spend hours every evening on the phone. Sometimes, I would stand there for several minutes and neither of us would say a thing. That might seem ridiculous, but it was nice to know that she was on the other end of the line.

This initial love feeling affects every part of the couple's life. She is all he thinks about. She cannot wait until the next day so they can be together again. What is this feeling? How can it be so strong? Why would someone be consumed by its power? Author Gary

Chapman explains it like this: "At its peak, the 'in love' experience is euphoric. We are emotionally obsessed with each other." Oxytocin is out the roof. When one person has a physical attraction to another, it triggers a feeling of love that will most likely facilitate a pursuit. This process starts off by the two becoming more acquainted. They might meet for coffee or go out to dinner. However, the motive is not just a great cup of java or some awesome food, but it is so much more—the motivation is an initial love feeling that causes someone to say, "This could be the one."

This feeling or experience takes a hold of the individual and seems to cause blindness. It gives meaning to the old adage, "*Love is blind.*" Her friend sees him as a jerk; she sees a cute and silly guy. His buddy says she is controlling and dictates his every move. He thinks she is gorgeous, and she wants to be with him every moment of every day. This feeling causes her to ignore his imperfections and flaws. She laughs at his quirks. He smiles at her jealousy. But don't get caught up in the clouds, and don't let these feelings of love put scales over your eyes so you can't see the faults or annoying quirks. It's okay to recognize the little things that annoy you. It's normal for a person to have qualities or personality temperaments that you don't really like. The relationship can still work out. It is not the end of the world. Either you will believe this person is not the one for you or you will see that no one is perfect, and you can learn to work through his or her weaknesses. By the way, you will never find a perfect mate, so stop looking and start pursuing.

The problem lies in the initial love experience that causes love blindness. You will have this feeling, but the feeling can be a problem if you don't understand some of its dynamics. One day, the initial love experience will be gone. I'm not talking about your love for that person disappearing; I'm referring to the initial love experience that we have at the onset of a relationship. This particular feeling will go away. It might go away in a year, maybe two. However, it will end. Here is where some couples fall apart. *"Oh no! I married the wrong person."* I have heard this statement many times, and it is not that you married the wrong person—it is that you begin to see your partner in his or her natural state through the lens of reality. He really does have bad breath in the morning. *"I don't ever remember his breath smelling that bad!"* She really does look different in the morning after she wakes up. *"You wouldn't believe what she looks like when she*

49

gets up. What happened to her face? I didn't sign up for this!"

When the feeling starts dwindling, reality sets in. He is the same person you dated. She is the same sweet person you used to text for hours. It's just that you are losing that initial love experience, and now it's time to start developing feelings of love. I believe that our Creator designed it this way for a reason. If you and I had not experienced these initial love feelings, some of us would still be looking for the perfect mate—and believe me, that person doesn't exist. Also, we tend to treat the one with whom we have this initial love experience so differently during the early days of dating. *"He can do no wrong." "She has very few flaws, if any." "That was so cute!" "It's okay; it's just her way." "Oh, he has the best family!"* But he does a lot of wrong things. She has many flaws. The family is not that good. That was not cute; in fact, it was disrespectful. The chemical in our brains allows more grace at the beginning of our relationships. If two people were to behave early in their relationship as they would after being married for a while, neither would continue the relationship. At some point, every person will be him or herself, but this initial love experience is to help "jump-start" the relationship. However, if all couples would act the way they did when their relationships first started, there would be fewer broken marriages.

Marital satisfaction is important if a couple wants to live a happy life full of fun moments. It would be miserable to live a long married life and not enjoy being together. I have seen many couples who are still married today, some over fifty years, who literally cannot stand to be in the same room together. Their life is horrible and miserable. Sadly, research has shown that many couples remain in their relationships and live this way. Marriage is not always full of perpetual bliss, but you can develop a happy, fulfilling relationship. According to Pamela Regan, in her book *The Mating Game: A Primer on Love, Sex, and Marriage*, "Longitudinal studies generally find that satisfaction declines steadily throughout marriage." Specifically, most couples begin their married lives with a "honeymoon" period characterized by a great deal of satisfaction and well-being. This progressively declines over the next several years, stabilizes for a time (often between the fourth and sixth years of marriage), and then either remains stable or continues to decline, assuming the couple stays together.

Why does this feeling go away? Even though we have a tendency to exaggerate our strengths and hide most of our weaknesses to impress the other person while dating, it is just a matter of time until our true colors will surface and we begin to see each other more realistically. Sometimes, I think I would like to see the world in fantasy instead of reality. It would make life much easier. However, it will never be that way. I believe that every individual should improve strengths and work on weaknesses. However, this takes time. I can't think of a better reason to work on my weaknesses than to become a better person for my wife, unless it was for spiritual purposes. Of course, it isn't enjoyable working on our flaws. Sometimes, I would rather my wife just laugh at some of my quirks instead of rolling her eyes and shaking her head or raising her eyebrows.

My wife has this thing she does when I do something ornery. She gives me a certain look and raises one eyebrow. I know that she is really serious when she raises both eyebrows at the same time. We have this running joke that I can make her raise her eyebrows on command. I get whacked in the arm when I say, "Wow! Every time you raise your eyebrows, the wrinkles around your eyes disappear." If she had three eyebrows, I believe I could get all three on that one. To get to the point in your marriage where both of you can have fun like this, it matters what you do in your relationship when things are going well. If you are not nurturing your relationship and doing what is necessary while everything is good, then when you want to be funny, but the relationship is in a bad place, nothing will be funny. During the early phases of the marriage, it is a great time to gain knowledge and learn how to take care of each other.

Just gaining knowledge is not the power that you need for your relationship. Knowledge is great! Premarital counseling along with the information you receive through that process is priceless. However, knowledge by itself is useless. Knowledge is not power; it is potential power. Information combined with application or action is power. If you learn ways of developing your marriage including techniques, approaches, tools, and methods but never apply them, it is just knowledge. But knowledge with application is true power. It is imperative to be intentional during the onset of the marital relationship to learn everything you can about your mate and how to continually create *love feelings* so that when the initial love experience is gone, you can now *create* moments instead of hoping they happen automatically.

In the town where I live, two industrial power plants supply electricity all over our state and beyond. I heard a concept from Brendon Burchard, a *New York Times* best-selling author and the world's leading high-performance coach. He stated that power plants do not just have electricity; they generate it. They take a source such as coal or natural gas and they generate electricity. In a marriage, after the initial love experience is gone, it is like electricity—you don't just have love feelings, you must generate them.

Brent Sharpe is a good friend of mine and a marital and family therapist. In his book, *The Making of a Marriage: Building Healthy, Whole People and Marriages that Last a Lifetime,* Brent states: "Behaviors of love do not follow the feelings of love. Feelings of love follow the behaviors of love." In other words, after the initial love experience is over, there will be times when you are not having *love feelings* toward your mate. Sometimes he will just tick you off and you will not be feeling the love. However, the masters of marital relationships generate love feelings, no matter how they feel. The situation doesn't matter; they still show love-communicating behaviors, which in turn generate love feelings.

Couples who do not recognize this early tend to lose their way in the marriage because they wonder, *"What happened?"* They say things like, *"I married the wrong person. How could I have not seen this?"* These little issues were there all the time; remember, love is blind. It doesn't matter who you marry. There will always be differences that cause disagreements in a relationship. Changing mates does not fix or eliminate the problem. The reason that changing your mate doesn't work is that you take *yourself* into the next relationship, and *you* don't change anything about *you*. Then the cycle starts all over again, and you will start believing that you married the wrong person again. Isn't it funny how we never look at ourselves as being part of the problem; it is always the other person? If you want your relationship to change, the first place to start is *you*. You must first be the change that promotes change in your relationship.

This is the moment in marriage where the work begins. It is where couples start creating love-communicating behaviors. They create *love moments* that are intentional. Now, love becomes a choice instead of being automatic like the initial love experience. Here is where individuals work on themselves instead of trying to change the other person. It is not that you married the wrong person; you just need to do the right things over a long period to nurture and cultivate the relationship. Zig Ziglar says it best: "It is far more important to be the right kind of person than it is to marry the right kind of person."

If you can understand that each person has flaws, and each person's role is to focus on each other's strengths, not the faults, you will start seeing the best in your mate. When you start seeing the good things in your spouse and avoid the tendency to focus on the shortcomings, it changes the environment of the relationship. The feelings of love will be more prevalent.

Andrew Carnegie, born in 1835, became one of the richest men in the history of America. His wealth was accumulated in the steel industry. In 1901, he sold the Carnegie Steel Company to banker John Pierpont Morgan for $480 million. That is a lot of money today, let alone in 1901. Carnegie viewed his wealth a lot differently than some. He was very generous, eventually giving away $350 million. That would be an equivalent of billions today. He established more than 2,500 libraries, gave many donations to churches, funded many organizations dedicated to the research of science (some still exist today), and he donated $1.1 million for the land and construction of the well-known Carnegie Hall, the legendary New York City concert venue that opened in 1891.

Over time, Carnegie had forty-three millionaires working for him. How can one person or one company be able to hire that many millionaires? He was asked this question by a reporter, and he explained that not all of them were millionaires when they joined the company, but they had in fact become millionaires while working for him. How did he develop such valuable men that he was willing to pay them enough to become millionaires? Carnegie said, "You develop people in the same way you mine for gold. When you mine for gold, you must literally move tons of dirt to find a single ounce of gold. However, you do not look for the dirt—you look for the gold." If you look so diligently for the dirt or flaws in your spouse, you will miss the gold. Your mate has the gold and strengths to meet your needs and help in your weaknesses. You have got to look past the faults and embrace the strengths.

Barry Mann and Cynthia Weil, the husband and wife song-writing team, penned the lyrics to the famous song, "You've Lost that Lovin' Feelin'." It became the most aired song on the radio, getting over eight million plays from the time it was released in 1964 until 2000. Here are the lyrics:

You never close your eyes anymore
When I kiss your lips
And there's no tenderness like before
In your fingertips.

You're trying hard not to show it
But baby, baby I know it.

You've lost that lovin' feelin'
Whoa, that lovin' feelin'
You lost that lovin' feelin'
Now it's gone, gone, gone, whoa-oh-oh.

I'll bet you were lip-syncing and singing the melody as you read it. No wonder it was one of the most played songs on the radio. Sing-along songs stick in your mind and become familiar. In fact, now that you've read this, you will call me names tomorrow because this song will still be in your head. Unfortunately, this song is so true in many marriages.

When the initial love experience is gone, if we do not become intentional about love-communicating behaviors, we will begin to see our love attributes wane that we once exhibited. She won't close her eyes anymore when you kiss. He won't hold your hand like before, if at all. You'll try to fake it, but the tension cannot be ignored. You've lost that lovin' feelin'. What do you do? It's simple: **GET IT BACK!** Can you really get back those loving feelings? I tell you emphatically, absolutely! But it takes intentionality. It does not matter whether you have felt those love feelings for a year, two years, or twenty years. If you have lost that lovin' feelin' that you once had for your mate, you can experience those feelings all over again. However, you must become intentional. It is not magic. There are no counselors, therapists, pastors, marital coaches, friends, or family members who can wave a wand over you and declare those feelings to return. It takes intentional, love-communicating inter-actions, practiced over and over and over for a long time.

I am giving you many different methods of devel-oping the behaviors that will ultimately transform your relationship so both of you will begin to show love and feel loved again. If you apply everything in this book, he will become your BFF all over again. She will once again be your BFF. But I must tell you this: it takes two. It takes both individuals doing the necessary behaviors to make it work. If only one of you is being intentional and the other is not, it will not work, and your marriage will not be transformed.

I met with a couple who was experiencing this very thing. Both husband and wife had been neglectful in showing their love for each other. They had gotten lax in doing intentional things. They were still doing some activities together side by side (ball games, church, kids' activities, family events, running errands, Christmas, and Thanksgiving), but their face-to-face times were rare. Those connecting moments of just hanging out, going on dates, taking a walk holding hands, sitting on the couch talking about their day, sitting on the back porch together and enjoying the view, talking about their hopes and dreams, eating dinner at home and sharing their day, or spending time laughing together were things of the past. They were non-existent.

Side-by-side activities will not get you closer relationally; they will get only the necessary life things done. It is the face-to-face interactions that will change your married life and help you grow closer. You and your spouse can lose your emotional and physical connection when you interact only side by side. Of course, the side-by-side duties must be done. They are not bad; however, they are not enough to keep you from drifting apart. Each week you must have some dedicated face-to-face time, and you must become intentional about it. It is much easier to focus on the side-by-side activities; they cry out much louder for your attention. In fact, sometimes you don't even have to think about them—they remind you. You do not have to write on your calendar that you need to shop for groceries. Your stomach will remind you. Or the kids will be screaming because you are out of Oreos: *"We have no food!"*

You do not have to be reminded to go to church. *"Oh, it's Sunday! Let's go to church."* However, it takes intentionality to come home from work and say, *"Let's sit down; I want to hear about your day"* or *"Let's take a walk together."* How about going on a date, sitting across from each other, putting the phones on silent, and talking about your hopes and dreams for your future? Ask your mate about her dream vacation. Talk about where you want to be in five, ten, twenty, or fifty years from now. Just DREAM together. Dr. John Gottman calls this building love maps.

Unfortunately, the couple that I mentioned above did not make it. They had gotten so far away from each other physically, emotionally, and relationally due to the neglect of the face-to-face priorities that she checked out. I have found that when one person checks out, it is usually impossible to mend and it's usually over. But it doesn't have to be. Refer to Chapter 2, "Change the Way You Think."

When the initial love experience is gone, it's time to create *love feelings*. Creating them can be fun and productive. I have heard people say, *"I don't know what she wants me to do to show her I love her."* I have this extremely well-thought-out, well-researched method of finding out from your mate what he or she wants. Here it is: **Just ask!** Ask your mate what you can do to show her that you love her. Ask him what he would like you to do to show him that you love him. Stop trying to read each other's mind and just ask. We are not mind-readers. Although, after being married for over thirty years, my wife and I will sometimes say the same thing at the same time. It's almost like we can read each other's mind. Now, that's a little scary! But we really can't, so the best way for me to know what she wants is to ask.

What does it look like to show love? Well, this can be different for everyone, but one thing for me is that I usually open the car door for my wife when we go somewhere. I know we live in a different world and a different culture that honors equality, and she can open the door just as easily as I can. Some may say, "Why doesn't she open it for you?" Okay, maybe I am a little old-fashioned, and maybe that was a gentlemanly way of showing respect to a female when I was growing up. I'm no respecter of persons; I'll hold open the door for anyone who is coming or going into a building. Maybe it is the way I grew up or my way of showing respect to my wife, but I believe it is one of the gestures that I use intentionally to show her how much I love her. It is something I want to do to for her. Take some advice from a person who has been married over thirty-three years: love-communicating gestures will take you places with your mate that you definitely want to go.

Zig Zigler says, "If you treat her like a thoroughbred, you'll never end up with a nag." That is some pretty good advice. He also says, "Treat him like a champ, and you'll never end up with a chump." There are times when we have a tendency to act like a nag or a chump, but everyone has bad days, right? However, if you learn to create love-communicating behavioral moments and to be intentional about showing your love for your spouse, you will develop a healthy relationship. Much of the stress from marital problems is not because of what we do, but because of what we don't do. The intensity of your marital conflict in the future is determined by what you do today. If you neglect love-communicating behaviors today while things are good, negative tension will begin to build, and when conflict arises, the intensity of the emotions for that moment will be higher. However, if you do the necessary things daily that enhance your relationship, when conflict does happen—and it will—resolution will go much more smoothly. Why would you not want to treat your BFF in this way?

My wife and I, while shopping, will occasionally have an argument, and at that moment, I'm not feeling a lot of love. When we head to the car I think, *"Should I open the car door for her or not?"* It would have been a lot easier to let her get in by herself. But I put aside my feelings and opened the car door anyway. When you love someone and you want the relationship to be topnotch, it is the love-communicating behaviors that let your mate know that you love him or her, no matter the situation. It doesn't matter whether we are in an argument or not; I still love her. Why would I not show it? I can be upset and still show her that I love her. It doesn't make the matter go away. There have been times when she was getting into the car while I was holding the door and I thought to myself, *"This would be a perfect opportunity to slam her leg in the car door"* and say, *"Oh, I am so sorry. I didn't mean to do that!"* I'm just joking—I would never do that. I have even joked with her about it, and yes, I get the raised eyebrows.

"I love you" is not something you can say just once at the beginning of your relationship and have it last a lifetime. In fact, love is more about actions than what a person says. In the Bible, the author James states that some will argue and say, "Some people have faith; others have good deeds. But I say, how can you show me your faith if you don't have any good deeds? I will show you my faith by my good deeds." I can say I love my wife, but if I don't show it, it doesn't mean much. I will show her my love by my deeds. Love runs out if we are not showing it intentionally every day.

Some things that you give your mate will cause love feelings to last longer than others. For instance, chocolate candy lasts about one day. You give her chocolate, and she will be excited for a day. However, you'd better have something to do or give her the next day because the feelings are short-lived. Flowers may last a day and a half or two; however, excitement about diamonds will last about a month. You can get some good points with diamonds! But this feeling will expire, too. In the same way, saying or showing *"I love you"* lasts only a short time. It runs out after a few hours. You must create a continuous habit of saying, *"I love you"* and showing your spouse that you love him or her through love-communicating behaviors.

I once had a tire on my car that kept losing air. I would put air in it and get the pressure back to the right amount (35 psi) to keep the indicator light satisfied. After a few days, it would be right back down and the light was back on. I would stop at an air station and add more. The problem was a constant leak that wasn't getting repaired. I kept doing just enough to bring it back up to the desired pressure, but it lasted only about one day. I kept putting a band-aid on it, but in just a little while, it was right back down. I wasn't intentional about fixing the problem. I would get distracted and forget. One day I went out to check the tire and it was completely flat. I had put it off so long that the leak got worse and eventually the tire wouldn't hold air at all.

If you continue to put air in a tire that has a leak or keep driving on a low tire, one day it will not be repairable. By putting a patch on your relationship just enough to get by, the time will come when you will forget or get too lax and the relationship will be flat or worse, unrepairable. The relationship will be in trouble. You can fill it back up and get a little more time, but it will come to the point where every time you check the tire, it will be flat. If you do not fix the problems in your relationship and just take things for granted, one day it may go flat and even worse, it will no longer be repairable. Love must be nurtured. Love-communicating behaviors are the fix that keeps the relationship healthy and alive.

Every one of us has a love bank. Men, I may start losing you when I get too mushy about your feelings, but you have a love bank as well. I believe men want to know that their wives love them. They may not want their buddies to know, but they want to know. Here is the thing about your personal love bank: there must be daily deposits. Since both you and your spouse need love, you will both be making withdrawals from each other's love bank. If you continue to make withdrawals and there are no deposits, your mate's love bank will overdraft. You will begin drawing more than what is in your spouse's account. You can't just continue to take and not make deposits. Both of you must deposit much more than you withdraw. No one can last for long on an empty love bank. So it is imperative that you both do some kind of love-communicating behavior consistently and make deposits into each other's love bank to keep the accounts full.

I am a nerd when it comes to budgeting, spreadsheets, and putting them together. I get a certain satisfaction when bills are paid and I log everything into the budget column. My wife and I use the free Every Dollar App created by Dave Ramsey and Ramsey Solutions. It is user friendly, and it automatically calculates our budget as I enter each line item. When we input our income and our bills are paid and entered, it automatically subtracts from the total, and it helps us maintain a zero-based budget. This app allows us to budget our debits and credits so that there are no discrepancies or worse yet, an overdraft in our bank account. However, we must be disciplined to keep up with the entries and not spend more than our budget allows. If we spend money and it is not designated in a budget line, that amount must be deducted from one of the other budget entries. Dave Ramsey calls this an envelope system. We created an envelope for each expense item and disperse the needed amount into each envelope until our income is fully allocated. Each dollar is assigned a certain envelope before the month begins and before anything is spent.

As income comes in, we spend the money and enter the data according to the budget. Again, if money is spent on something that is not in the budget, we must assign that amount to another envelope. If not, the bank account will not match the budget and the account will overdraft. In other words, we created a plan for success with our money. Being intentional with love-communicating behaviors is like setting up a budget—a relationship budget.

Certain things are essential in a relationship. Let's call them line items or *needs*. We all have *needs*, and we have only a certain amount of time. In fact, we all have twenty-four hours each day. No one has more or less, and when it's gone, we don't get it back. Let's say time is the *income*. There is only a certain amount, and we have to budget it and appropriate it according to how much we have and to the places (envelopes) that are most important.

You must budget *time* to your mate in many areas of your relationship, and one of those areas is love-communicating behaviors. If you allocate a certain amount of time to these behaviors but spend it somewhere else, love-communicating behaviors get cut back or completely out. Remember, in an envelope system, there is only a certain amount of money, and the only way to spend more is to make more and bring in more income. This works great in a financial budget, but unfortunately, in a *time budget*, you cannot make more time. So, when you spend time outside of your *time budget*, in another envelope, you can't make it up.

This might work for a while, but eventually, your mate's love bank will suffer, and the relationship will become bankrupt. I have coached many couples where this sort of thing happened until a spouse became emotionally and relationally bankrupt to the point of failure. He or she couldn't survive the rejection. The love bank account was empty for so long that the account was closed. What I have discovered in these types of relationships is that there is usually no recovery. Too much damage has been done, and the bankrupt spouse is done and has checked out of the relationship.

In a later chapter I will be covering an ideal of creating a culture of unconditional grace in the home. This is offering grace, no matter the situation. However, a person can handle only so much rejection before enough is enough. How long can anyone hold out? It is different for every person, but I believe there is a point where many attempts are made to communicate basic relational needs and the other party continues to neglect the empty love bank account. This is a recipe for failure.

I have counseled some couples where the offender finally realized he or she was not meeting the other's needs and would notice that the spouse was checking out. The offender would immediately ask forgiveness and start the process of doing what was necessary. But the other party was done and wanted no part of reconciliation. Here is where unconditional grace must be practiced. I understood that this had gone on for a long time and it took awhile for the person to realize there was a problem. But marriage is about forgiveness and grace. Sometimes we must put the past behind us and start a process of healing. We'll talk more about forgiveness and trust in another chapter, but I need to indicate here that trust is different from forgiveness. Trust takes longer to develop, while forgiveness might be able to happen much more quickly. We can forgive yet not completely trust and can still build the relationship.

This is really about changing yourself. Sometimes your mate will do things that are not right and that are hurtful to the relationship. It may take your spouse some time to come around to changing. But you *cannot* change your mate. You can only change yourself. When you realize that you can change only who you are and what you do, it will take the burden off of you to change your spouse. It is okay to complain about being treated unfairly. I will cover this more in another chapter, but complaining is different from criticism. A legitimate complaint helps the other person understand that there is an issue that must be solved. This requires a hard conversation.

While you were experiencing initial love feelings, you may have done some things that were goofy or even ridiculous. However, when the initial love experience is gone, you may do some really messed up, ridiculous, and sometimes hurtful and damaging things to your relationship. How do you solve this and create a life-long loving relationship with your BFF? You must learn to be consistent and intentional in displaying love-communicating behaviors to show that you love your mate. In the appendix you will find a love-communicating behaviors exercise for each of you to complete and start to the process of meeting each other's love needs and help keep the love bank full.

4

Personal Development

"Improving yourself is the first step in
improving everything else."
(Unknown)

I WOULD NOT want to write a book on marriage and friendship without including one of the most significant aspects of maintaining a healthy and satisfying relationship. What if you wanted to enhance your friendship with your BFF but you didn't know about an element that could ultimately change the trajectory of your marriage? Wouldn't you want to know what it was? Of course, you would. That is what this section is all about. This element might be overlooked or left out of some marriage books. However, I feel that it very important. What is it? Some might guess communication. Yes, communication is important, and I will address this later. Could it be intimacy? Intimacy is extremely important and necessary. The particular factor I am referring to is more about each individual rather than the two collectively. I am referring to *personal development.*

My wife and I often look at our marital relationship through the lens of the two of us as a whole; however, marriage has much to do with us as individuals. Yes, your marriage is about the two of you. It is about the both of you fulfilling your roles in the relationship and building your friendship. It does take two to tango. However, if I just focus on what my wife needs in the marriage and she just focuses on what I need, we lose sight of what needs to happen in us personally and our responsibility to ourselves. I need to focus on my own personal development before I begin to concentrate on what I need to be for my wife.

Many times I've seen an individual get so caught up in a relationship trying to please the other person that his or her own needs are neglected. I am not talking about selfishness but about personal development. It matters that you are healthy personally. Improving yourself is the first step in improving everything else. I will show you some facets that I believe you will need to nurture personally so you can be everything you can be for your mate and will be able to face anything in your marriage.

Personal development is an element in your marriage that your spouse cannot do for you. I realize that there may be personal health challenges, but ultimately, no one can cause you to grow personally except you. Marital health and your friendship with your mate are about what you do for each other, but it is just as much about what you do for yourself and who you become as an individual. Who you become is solely dependent upon you. No one can change you, and you cannot change anyone else.

There are four things that will help you become the BFF that your mate needs you to be in your relationship. I will show you some overlooked personal developmental strategies for your marriage that will not only transform you personally and make you a better person but will also allow you to become the kind of person that your wife or husband dreams about.

Picture this. Your wife is out with her girlfriends getting a pedi and mani, and she spends the entire time bragging about you and how awesome you are. She is so annoying, and her friends can't believe that a marriage can be this great and that a husband can be that wonderful. Or your husband is out with his buddies, and they say things like, "Dude, stop already. Stop talking about your trophy wife. You seriously cannot have a wife this good. All a wife does is nag and demand us to change!" You smile and think, *I am one lucky man to have a wife like mine.* If you will just lean in to these four personal development strategies, your marriage will be better than you could ever think or imagine.

1. Become a Better You

I will say this over and over: If you want things to change around you, you must change first. I wish that I had a dollar for every husband and wife that has come into my office expecting each other to change. I would be very wealthy! So many people let the circumstances around them determine how they act or react. I had a guy come to me recently who complained for an hour about his job, his marriage, his kids, his dad, and many other things around him as causing the problem of not advancing in his job, marriage, and life. He even got emotional and cried as he blamed everything and everyone for not being a success. His list went on and on, but one major thing was missing: *he* wasn't on the list.

No matter how diligently we try, we do not have control over circumstances, issues, and the people around us. Difficulties will happen. Circumstances will arise. People will do things that we have no control over. Jim Rohn says that life is like seasons—you will experience summer, winter, fall, and spring. Winter comes every year. Some winters are bad, and some are not so bad, but winter is coming. But spring always comes after winter, so hold on, spring is coming. What is the key to handling all of this? It is not whether you will face something difficult or not, but it is what you do and who you become when you face them. It matters who you become under adverse situations.

Let's suppose your spouse does not do exactly what you want. How you respond matters. What if he comes home from work, goes straight to his easy chair, does not talk to you, and just ignores you? What would be your response? "I would jump right in the middle of him and line him out!" What if he has had a tough day at work and needs to decompress for a few moments before he can focus and give you the attention you need? What if you became a supporter instead of a complainer? "Well, he shouldn't act like that!" Maybe so, but your behavior will determine the outcome in the next few minutes. Change begins in you. Your decisions will set the pace for your actions. You will react to how you interpret the circumstances in the next few moments. Your beliefs in that moment will determine your actions.

Now, back to the story about the person who listed everyone and everything but himself as the cause for his lack of success. He was using blame to try to become successful. But blame and habitual complaining are not strategies. I believe that everyone needs to complain at times. Complaining is different than criticism. Criticism attacks the person, and complaining attacks the problem. You should be able to speak your complaints to your mate in love to communicate what you need. However, I am referring to constant complaining about everyone else being the cause for your failures and never taking any responsibility. In this example, the man tried to blame everyone and everything as his problem. There will always be someone else we can blame, and there will always be circumstances to blame as well. When our reactions are based on people around us or our surroundings, our mood and behaviors will be all over the place. However, when you can look at yourself as the first one to change, not only will the problem change around you, but how you view the issue will also change. So be the change and become a better you!

How do you do this? It can be so frustrating when change around you involves more than just you. There will be times when you change and become better, but the situation will not completely change until the other party changes as well. Take your marriage, for instance—it takes both of you changing to make your marriage work. One person cannot make the necessary changes and the other live haphazardly in the relationship. When only one is making the sacrifices of change while the other is refusing to change, this leads to a hard conversation, and if there is no hard conversation, then there will be trouble. This is where a person needs to speak the truth in love. Just ensure that before you complain about your mate not making necessary changes, you must examine your life completely to make sure you are making the essential changes in you.

You may say, "What if nothing changes? What if my spouse doesn't change?" We often see many changes that need to take place in our mates, but we see only a few in us. I have seen many individuals who, before marriage, never even notice the many quirks that the boyfriend or girlfriend had. In fact, when they did, they seemed so cute. But after a while, into the marriage, these things became so annoying that one spouse would become furious with the other. They will say things like, "Why can't you be more like me?" At the onset of the marriage, the differences may not be a problem, but later, they become annoyances. I always tell couples, "If you wanted to marry someone just like you, you should have married yourself!" The differences are what make the BFF marital relationship unique and an adventure. I can't even imagine my wife being just like me. Even though I don't understand her sometimes, I love her diversity. I just need to be the best version of myself for her.

How do you become the best version of who you are?

Love Yourself First

I hear some individuals who are so self-conscious that they become overwhelmed with personal insecurities. They look in the mirror and hate the way they look. I get it! Many times in my life I have hated my weight or my hairstyle, and during the formative years of my life, I used to look in the mirror and wonder how anyone could like or love me. I was not a very popular kid in school. My dad was a pastor, and we moved a lot. In fact, out of the twelve years of grade school, middle school, junior high, and high school, I attended thirteen different schools. I didn't go to kindergarten, so that was thirteen different schools from first grade until I graduated from high school. That is a lot of moving and trying to make friends.

I was not good at sports. I was not a good student when it came to grades. In high school, I did the bare minimum to graduate. I think I finished with a two-point-something grade-point average, maybe less. Whatever it was, I had the minimum to graduate. I just didn't have a mindset of becoming much in my life or thinking that I was anything special. I really didn't like myself. It was when I graduated from high school that this way of thinking began to change. I wish I could tell you that I found a mentor who taught me what I am teaching you now. That was not what happened. When I got away from all of the popular people, I started to realize that popularity wasn't the important thing. It was being who I was created to be and using my talents and abilities that I was given.

Guess what—those popular kids in junior high and high school lost their popularity when they hit college. How things change when you get out of high school and you get older. Now, your hair doesn't care about flowing in the wind as it did when you were in high school; it just falls out. Your metabolism doesn't say, "You were really popular in high school, so I will make sure that you are always slim and irresistible." It slows down, your fat cells fill up, and next thing you know, you have a belly that grew overnight or your hips have exploded with growth instantly. As life goes on, it is easy to not love yourself.

I have learned that for me to be everything I need to be for my wife, I have to love myself first. I have to be okay with who I am. Of course, I want to change some things about myself. However, I have come to realize that I must look in the mirror every day and know that the person I see is the perfect version of who I am. If I don't like some things about that person in the mirror, I can still say, "You are the perfect version of me today, but tomorrow there are some things I need to change."

You must look in the mirror right now and say, "You are the perfect version of you today!" But you may say, "I don't like how I look. I need to lose weight." It's okay if you want to make some changes in your life, but if you can't love who you are right now, you won't be able to love who you will become when you are twenty pounds lighter. There will always be something that you don't like.

I have seen individuals who create many problems in marriage because of insecurities. They have made themselves believe that *"If I can't love me, then how can my spouse love me? If I can't stand to look at myself in the mirror, my spouse will not be able to look at me either."* No matter how much he validates you, you just can't believe him. No matter how much she adores you just the way you are, you have problems loving yourself; you can't believe she can see you any differently than you see yourself.

My wife was the one who helped me break out of my self-pity insecurities. She has loved me through all of my hang-ups, bad days, insecurities, and failures. On days that I feel as if what I do is not making a difference, she will just let me vent, and then she will validate me. I must see myself the way she does. I must believe in me the way she does. I must be the person she believes me to be. Love yourself no matter what, and you will see a difference in your marriage.

Change for Her; Change for Him

After loving who you are today and making the necessary changes that you want for yourself, the next step is making some changes for your mate. You may say, *"My man likes me the way I am!"* or *"She loves me just the way I am!"* Yeah, I get it. He is crazy about you.

She thinks you are all that. However, I know from being in the room with many couples, your spouse would like to see changes in you. Many marriages that are in the early stages may not believe this statement. They are so much in love that they can't even see the flaws just yet.

I know a couple who have been married almost two years, and the husband and wife are together nearly everywhere. That's not a bad thing. It will most likely change some day, but it's good for now. I do see some minor conflicts in them, and it's comical. One thing that she hates is that he sometimes doesn't have enough deodorant on, and she thinks he smells. She will go up to him and take a big sniff of his armpit and give him that look and say, "You need to put on some deodorant." His reply: "I use a 24-hour deodorant, and it hasn't been 24 hours yet!" Some of the things they say are hilarious, but I want couples like this to know that as time goes on, these things will not be funny anymore. She thinks it's funny now, but at the same time she is serious. He will eventually have to change, and he should for her.

I met with an incredible couple for premarital coaching recently. She has been married before, but he hasn't, and they are in love and will have a great life together. We covered many things about marriage, but one particular problem surfaced. It was an issue to him, and she couldn't understand why it bothered him so much. He was adamant about her changing this part of her life since they would be married in a few weeks. She was resistant about the change, and I could see that it was going to be a problem in the relationship. We discussed many different ways of managing, coping, or changing. I did not give them the answer to the problem. It was not my position to give them the answer as much as coaching them through the problem. However, in this particular situation, she was going to have to change some for him, and he was adamant. Why should she have to change? Well, this particular thing was a must for him to feel secure in her being his BFF. Even though she was still having difficulty in understanding, it was a big deal to him, and this was where she would have to change for him. Some things are not bad in a sense, but they are just not beneficial.

Some wives might say, "I should not have to change this for him!" Maybe so, but are you willing to allow a seemingly simple thing to become a barrier with your spouse, or can you just say, "I'll change for you!" What is it that might be causing a conflict in your marriage that you don't want to change? Are you willing for this to become a barrier from now on just to hang on to it?

I know a guy who while dating, would go out with girls just to discover they drink alcohol, and he was totally in contrast to this. One of his dates became so upset at him after he stopped the relationship because she was not willing to give it up. It's not that he didn't like her or that he treated her badly for her choices. He simply told her that he was totally against it and that he would not continue building a relationship on those terms. Good for him to not let the relationship continue, knowing that this was a marriage deal breaker for him. Many times, couples continue thinking that the other person will change after the marriage. Let me give you some good advice: this normally does not happen, and it will turn into a battle.

Becoming a better you might be the very thing that transforms your relationship. It is easy to think it's the other person changing that will make it better. Your BFF is worth making some changes. Becoming a BFF is just as important as having a BFF. Make the necessary changes and watch your relationship soar.

2. Sleep Your Way to a Great Marriage

Yes, I am going to talk about sleep. You may ask, "What in the world does this have to do with my BFF and this book?" I am so glad you asked! I believe I am an evangelist for teaching people how to get good quality sleep, and I will show you how sleeping, or not sleeping, is affecting your marriage and relationship. I have done a lot of research on sleep. I became interested when I found myself always tired, no matter how much sleep I was getting.

Quality sleep is huge when it comes to personal development. No one can sleep for you. I know this sounds foolish, but getting good quality sleep is all on you. There is a difference between getting sleep and getting good quality sleep. I have heard many people say, "I slept for eight hours, but I still feel tired!" You may sleep for twelve hours, but it does not mean that you slept well. Here is the number one answer that I hear from people when I ask them, "How are you doing?" The number one response: "I'm tired!" Our whole country is tired. Everybody is tired. I am not making light of this. I do not believe they are just making conversation; people are truly tired. So how important is sleep? Well, according to most of the population, it must not be that important; people are not getting good quality sleep, and they are tired.

Let's put some things in perspective for a moment. According to a study by the Michigan Transplant Center, oxygen is very important. I don't think I need a study to tell me this. If you cut my oxygen off, I'll fight somebody to get it back. This study shows that after one minute without air, brain cells begin to die, but life is possible. After three minutes without oxygen, brain damage is likely, and after ten minutes, many brain cells have died and the person is unlikely to recover. After fifteen minutes without oxygen, it is virtually impossible to recover. I would say that oxygen is number one on the list of things that are important.

As you probably guessed, the second thing in order of importance is water. On average, a person can live only about three days without water. According to one 1979 article, an eighteen-year-old Austrian man by the name of Andreas Mihavecz survived eighteen days without water when the police accidentally left him in a holding cell. However, it is a little fuzzy, because he allegedly licked condensation off the walls of the prison. But nevertheless, water is the second most important thing in life.

Another important thing we need is food. Some of us have plenty, and it shows. But within twenty-one days, a person needs to be eating something. In the ancient book, some people were going without food for forty days, fasting for spiritual purposes. I am sure this was a supernatural thing. I have heard of some people who have fasted for spiritual purposes for twenty-one days. I have done that, but it wasn't a complete fast. I ate certain things that gave me nourishment while I deprived myself from some delicacies. However, we do need food.

Is food the third most important thing we need to sustain us? Food was probably your third choice, but it is not. Food happens to be fourth on the list. First oxygen, second water, and third is sleep. Yes, sleep is more important than food. According to the sleep doctor, Dr. Michael Brues, the average person can go only nine days without sleep. The record is eleven days, but after nine days, the brain starts dying. The sleep-deprived person may be walking around and appear to be functioning somewhat, but won't be aware of anything that is happening.

Let me break this down. Oxygen is the number one thing we need to survive, and water is number two. However, even though we are not going to go very long without something to eat, food is not number three. Sleep is the third most important thing in your life for survival. You can go without food longer than you can go without sleep. Sleep is extremely important for your life and for your marriage.

I want to debunk a myth about sleep. You may have heard that the average person sleeps eight hours. You may say, "Yeah, right! I wish I could get eight hours." Well, this is a myth. The average person goes through five cycles of four stages and REM sleep each night, and the average cycle is approximately ninety minutes long. That is 450 minutes divided by 60, which equals 7.5 hours. The average person sleeps an average of 7.5 hours each night. There are exceptions to the rule—some require a little more and some a little less. It is not how much sleep you get per se, but how much your body needs.

You might be thinking, "I bought a book for my marriage, not a program on telling me how to sleep." But if you are not sleeping well, it will affect everything about your life, especially your marriage. The lack of quality sleep causes irritability, and it affects cognitive processes such as attention, alertness, concentration, reasoning, and problem solving. It also kills your sex drive, makes you forgetful, and impairs your judgment. All of these things can lead to marital conflict or inhibit working through marital issues effectively. So this is why I am an advocate of getting good quality sleep when it comes to marriage coaching. Most Americans are not getting good quality sleep.

What if the lack of getting good quality sleep is causing most of your arguing? Maybe she is not angry or upset at you; she is just sleep deprived and irritable. Once the arguing starts, then one problem after the other surfaces, and both of you begin what I call *conflict stacking*. Now, you can't even remember the original reason you started arguing, and you can't stand to be in the same room together. And on top of all of this, you have not had sex in several days, and this begins to add even more pressure to the relationship. All because you both are sleepy. Now do you see why getting good quality sleep is so important for your marriage?

How do you fix this? How do you get better sleep? You still have to get up, go to work, take care of the kids, go to all of their activities, go to church, mow the yard, clean the house, do laundry, and the list goes on and on. Yes, these things must be done, but you still need good sleep, right? You may say, "If I just had more time, I could get better sleep." But there is no more time. You must be strategic and plan your sleep schedule. I am going to give you a few suggestions that will set your evening for some great Zs. Some of these things happen throughout the day, which will begin to prepare you for your evening of good quality sleep.

Be Consistent with Going to Bed and Getting Up

A regular schedule will create a pattern so that your body will adjust and develop a habit of waking and sleeping. When a person is sporadic about going to bed and inconsistent about getting up, the body will never adjust, and good sleep will not happen. This is extremely difficult for those who do shift work, but even with working odd hours, one can get into a routine of consistent waking and going to sleep. There are routines for those who work nights and sleep during the day that need to be implemented to mock sleeping during the night. Three things to consider here: keep the room as dark as possible, maintain a room temperature between 63 and 68 degrees Fahrenheit, and use some sort of noise machine to block out daytime noises. These factors are important for night-time sleeping as well, but they are crucial for sleeping during the day.

How You Start Your Day Will Affect Your Sleep at Night

One of the best routines you can do to promote good sleep at night, especially getting to sleep, has to do with the first thing you do when you get up. First, get some sunlight immediately if possible. Getting a good dose of sunlight, or any light, will raise your cortisol levels and set your circadian rhythm for the day. Our bodies have a natural rhythm of wakefulness and sleep according to when the sun comes up and goes down, and getting sunlight the first thing in the morning helps set this rhythm. Also, getting exercise or some sort of movement, first thing, will help cortisol levels to rise at the desired rate. I'll discuss exercise shortly.

Along with sun and exercise, drink water first thing, at least 16 to 20 ounces. During the night, we lose at least a bottle of water through breathing so we wake up dehydrated. Starting the day hydrated will set you up for a great day of health. Your body will function as it should, and the daily rhythm will not be disturbed.

Limit Caffeine

Stop all consumption of caffeine by 2:30 or 3:00 P.M. Caffeine has a six- to eight-hour half-life, which means that your body will digest only half of the caffeine in six to eight hours. In other words, if you consume one cup of coffee, which has approximately 100 milligrams of caffeine, after six to eight hours, you will still have 50 milligrams of caffeine in your system. After another six to eight hours, you will still have 25 milligrams of caffeine in your system. Getting as much caffeine as you can out of your system before going to bed will help you get the necessary Zs your body needs. So how does this work?

In your system you have a chemical called adenosine, which plays an important role in the body. It slows down the activity of neurons. Throughout the day, it gradually builds up in the pineal gland in your brain, and toward the evening it causes you to start feeling sleepy. This suppression of nerve cell activity is what causes the feeling of drowsiness. However, adenosine is only one molecule different from caffeine, and it goes to the same area of the brain. When caffeine is present, adenosine is inhibited and it will not allow the body to get sleepy. Caffeine does not wake you up—that's cortisol's job. Caffeine keeps you from getting sleepy. Even if you are able to go to sleep, caffeine inhibits the body from getting good quality sleep because of the disturbance of melatonin, also produced and secreted in the pineal gland.

Some will supplement with over-the-counter melatonin to promote better sleep. Melatonin is the hormone in your system that keeps you asleep throughout the night. It works together with adenosine, which makes you sleepy; melatonin keeps you asleep. Your body produces all of the melatonin you need without any supplements—that is, if you use every means possible to allow it to concentrate in the system. Restricting caffeine early in your day will stimulate some of the best sleep you have ever experienced.

Turn Off All Technical Devices Thirty Minutes to One Hour Before Lights Out

Another inhibitor of sleep is blue light. Devices such as TV, phones, computers, etc., give off blue light, which suppresses melatonin in your system. The last thing you want is something keeping you awake when you are exhausted, and blue light will do this very thing.

How can you fix this problem? The best way is to shut down these devices thirty minutes to one hour before bedtime. This allows melatonin to rise in your system. If you must be on your phone later in the evening, set the brightness on your phone to cut out the blue light. You can go to your "Systems" under "Display and

Brightness" and click on "Night Shift" and schedule your phone to automatically shift the colors of your display to the warmer end of the spectrum. If you intend to watch TV until bedtime, get some blue blocker glasses to cut out the blue light. These techniques will allow melatonin to rise, and you can fall asleep and rest peacefully.

Stay in Bed All Night

One of the worst things you can do during the night is get up and move around. When you do this, the hormone cortisol begins to rise and forces melatonin to decrease. Melatonin and cortisol work together during the night. Around midnight, melatonin falls and cortisol rises. When cortisol is at a certain level and melatonin is at a lower level, cortisol will bring you out of unconsciousness and wake you up. However, if you get up and move around too much during the night, cortisol will rise, and you will have difficulty going back to sleep. So, no midnight snacks! Stay in bed! However, when you wake up in the morning, get up immediately and move around. The sooner you move around, the quicker your cortisol levels will rise so you will become wide awake. You will find that when you allow adenosine, melatonin, and cortisol to adjust naturally, you will get amazing sleep.

Exercise

Exercise not only promotes good health, but it is also another great activity for good sleep. According to some studies, if you exercise early in the day, even the first thing in your day, it allows you to sleep better a night. I know that "exercise" is a bad word to some, so let's change it to *movement*. One thing to keep in mind is to not exercise too late in the evening due to cortisol levels remaining high and inhibiting melatonin. In the latter part of your evening, you want cortisol dropping and melatonin rising, and movement is counterproductive to this.

Movement helps control body weight; combats health conditions and diseases such as stroke, high blood pressure, type 2 diabetes, depression, anxiety, many types of cancer, and arthritis; improves mood and boosts energy; and puts a spark back into your sex life. So yes, I believe exercise or movement is very important to your sleep and marriage.

Again, I believe that good quality sleep is so important that I have made it a major part of this book. Conflict is inevitable, and couples must learn to argue correctly and strategically. This is impossible if someone is sleep deprived. What if your marriage is on the brink of failure, and the way you can get it back on track is to be able to reason, communicate, confront the issue at hand, and talk through your problems effectively and efficiently? What if a lack of sleep is causing you to fail at these? This is in your control. Work on getting good quality sleep.

3. Spirituality

The third factor that I want to discuss concerning personal development is spirituality. I believe that we are all spiritual beings. There is a spiritual element to every person's life. You may not see spiritual things the same way I do. I am very adamant and serious about my spiritual life, but I don't try to force people to believe the same way I do. If I am in the right setting, I will share what I believe because my spirituality is extremely important to me, and I feel every person's decision matters for eternity. Your spiritual journey may not be like mine, but every person is a spiritual being.

Spiritual practices help promote peace, understanding, patience, tension relief, and empathy. These practices will stimulate a good relationship with your mate. Some of your most stressful moments in your marriage, including conflict, require some type of release technique to calm you and bring your heart rate back into alignment, lower your blood pressure, and take you from a state of psychological tension to psychological rest. Whatever psychological state that you are in will determine your behaviors.

I have developed a stress-relief process that I call a Spiritually Motivated Anxiety Release Technique (S.M.A.R.T.). I use this technique in many situations in which I might develop stress, anxiety, or lack of patience. To practice S.M.A.R.T., put on some sort of soft music without lyrics and begin a process of meditation. The meditation consists of clearing your mind from anything that might distract you or keep you at a state of psychological tension. However, just to clear your mind is not enough. This process includes concentrating on positive things while doing a breathing exercise. I have Bible verses that I focus on, but you might have some positive and motivating quotes that you can use for this activity.

First, I escape to a quiet place where I can be alone. While the music is playing, I take in a deep breath for four seconds and hold it for seven seconds. Then I release the breath for eight seconds and repeat this process eight to ten times. Taking deep breaths, holding them, and then releasing will allow endorphins to concentrate in the system, giving a calming effect. Continue by listening to the music; reading Scripture, positive quotes, or some other uplifting and motivating content; and allowing the stress to subside and bring your body to a state of rest and your mind to a place of psychological relaxation. S.M.A.R.T. is very effective when the couple is escaping the marital dance of conflict, and allows each to find a place of psychological rest and to be able to return and find resolution.

4. You Are Whole Alone

I believe to have a healthy marriage requires that each person is healthy and whole personally. You are whole by yourself, or you should be. Some may not believe that or even see it right now, but you do not need someone else to complete you. Read this again: YOU DO NOT NEED SOMEONE ELSE TO COMPLETE YOU! It seriously annoys me when I hear someone say, "He [or she] completes me." If he or she completes you, then if that person is not around you or does not exist, you just bounce around in la-la land running into walls and being lost.

Think about this for a moment. You have only one leg, one arm, one ear, one eye, and half a brain, and you are literally cut in half down the middle. Now you are walking around trying to function and find your second half to complete you. Can you imagine how ridiculous this would look? I know this seems absurd, but this is what I think when someone says, "He completes me." I get it—if something tragic happened to my wife, I would be so lost because she has an incredible role in my life. However, I could still function as a person. I would still go on in life. It would hurt for quite some time, but I would make it. I am whole without her. She is whole without me. She would continue in life if something happened to me.

This is a huge problem in many marriages today. Some believe that they would not make it without their spouses, and so much pressure is put on their mates to be more than they can be for the relationships, and they become smothering to the point that it causes marital problems. There is about 10 percent that your spouse cannot be for you. You might even put 100 percent of what you need on your mate. This is a huge amount of pressure. It will lead to one of you feeling like a failure. Don't put this kind of pressure on your mate. There are other people who can fulfill the 10 percent. Now, I am not talking about intimacy or infidelity. Your spouse should be the only one you are intimate with, and this includes physical, mental, and emotional. I am referring to things that other people in your life can do to support other needs.

I love to go camping. At least once a year, I will spend a week with my buddies camping. I load down a sixteen-foot trailer with everything but the kitchen sink and stay in a tent for a week. I actually have a portable kitchen sink that I take with me, though. My wife says that I have more kitchen items in my camping stuff than what she has in her kitchen. It is ridiculous what I take camping with me. Just recently we went on a camping trip, and I took a truckload of firewood. Within six days, we burned up every piece. I also should mention that it was 100 degrees. Hey, you can't go camping without a perpetual campfire, right? My wife will literally look at my truck and trailer, roll her eyes, and say, "This is ridiculous!" I just smile and say, "Yep!"

My wife refers to my style of camping as *glamping*. I get a campsite with electricity, and I run a high-powered fan 24/7. So it is not so primitive, but it's my style, and I am not giving up every luxury. Even though I do have some modern amenities, I do all of my cooking on outdoor stoves, cast iron pots, and other outdoor devices. It is one of the most phenomenal weeks of the year for me. But my wife does not like this style of camping at all. If we had a luxury home-on-wheels—that is, a camper with its own facilities—she'd be all in, but not a tent. It can be 100 degrees outside, and I am just as content as can be. She would complain, as she has before when I took her with me.

Some people will ask, "Why don't you ask your wife to go?"

I say, "I don't want her going with me on this trip."

"That's rude," they will say. But the one or two times that she has gone with me, I spent the entire time worried about whether she was comfortable or not. Any time she camps with me the way I love to, I can assure you that she is NOT comfortable.

The last time she went, it was around the end of July or beginning of August, which is the hottest and most humid time of the year in our area. It could be 95 to 100 degrees, but it would feel 10 degrees hotter because of the humidity. In spite of the heat, I had a fire going the entire time. My wife was miserable. I was in paradise, and she just didn't get it. It wasn't just the daylight hours that were miserable for her. My tent has two rooms—one in the back and the other by the zippered front door. My normal place to sleep is in the back room, and the front room by the door is for my excess equipment. When I got the tent set up, I started setting up my cot and showed her where she could set hers, in the front by the door. This was not going to work! She said, "What if someone comes in the tent. I don't want to be the first person to get mugged!" So I had to switch rooms with her, which completely messed up my entire routine. This was just the beginning of the night.

We went to bed between 9:30 and 10:00 P.M. By midnight she was in my room shaking me, waking me up to walk with her to the restrooms so she could pee. This continued throughout the night, at least five times. The next morning, I told her something had to change. Well, it did. We set up a new method of her using the bathroom. I'll just leave it at that.

Needless to say, the next time she went with me, we joined a friend of mine and his family, and we stayed in a huge fifth-wheel camper with its own bathroom, shower, kitchen, and air conditioning. This changed every-thing; she was a happy camper. But this is not my way of camping. In fact, when I go with this same buddy of mine who owns the camper, he stays in the camper and I stay in my tent.

This is something in my life that my wife cannot fulfill for me, but my buddies can. There are other things somewhat like this that my wife cannot do for me, but she lets me go on my own or with friends so that I can enjoy those parts of my life. I have dealt with many couples who think they must spend every moment with each other doing everything together to make their marriages work. On the other side of this, some couples spend so much of their time doing activities apart that it leads to other problems. Couples need to do some things individually, but it matters that they cultivate together-ness as well. You are whole without your mate, but it is fulfilling to nurture closeness and allow your mate to add to your life.

Several years ago, I worked in an industrial plant that made anhydrous ammonia, among several different fertilizers. We worked twelve-hour shifts, and I spent a lot of time with my coworkers. Most everyone I worked with was a hunter or fisherman, which helped turn me into one as well. This was the early stages of our marriage. In fact, seven months after I landed the job, we got married. I was fishing every day I had off. I would get off of a twelve-hour shift, after working all night, and head to the lake. I would fish all day and come home about the time my wife got home from work, which meant I could be up over thirty hours without sleep. Well, as soon as dinner was over and we sat down to watch some TV, guess what I did? Yes, I was out, sound asleep in my chair, while she watched TV alone. Most of my coworkers did the exact same thing. Our wives just learned to live with it. Some couples ended up divorced because of it. The ten percent of time alone is healthy, but spending the majority of one's time with friends or spending time in a way that keeps you from your spouse will eventually be detrimental to your marriage.

I learned quickly that this type of married lifestyle was not going to work, and taking my wife to a movie on date night and falling asleep would not cut it, which happened more than once. She was extremely patient with me, but I changed. However, many of my coworkers never changed. They did what they wanted and needed personally, which is okay to a point, but a marriage will not be healthy if spouses don't give ninety percent of their lives to each other.

To develop personally, you must first understand that you are whole without your spouse. You also must learn to balance your wholeness with giving the part of you that your mate needs to transform your BFF relationship.

However, understand that you are whole alone, and you can be for *you* all that *you* need to be while being all that you can be for your spouse so your friendship will grow stronger.

5

Marriage Success

"Marriage success is more about face-to-face moments
rather than side-by-side."
(Ronnie Gaines)

AS MUCH AS success is your goal for your marriage, sometimes the success of a marriage can be the very thing that causes failure. Let me explain what I mean. Of course, success is the goal, but I have seen many couples get so caught up in successful marriages that within just a few years, they were divorced. What would cause a great marriage to suddenly end? They seemed to be the perfect couple. It appeared that everything was going great. Every time they were in public, they seemed happy, they were doing well financially, the kids seemed happy, they were in church every week, and they appeared to be content and satisfied. In fact, they were the perfect couple that most would use as an example. Then, all at once, it was over. Well, it seemed to be all at once from the outside. However, after hearing their story, it was not. Things were happening that no one knew about, and over time, the relationship fell apart.

I know a couple who had been married for several years and appeared to have a happy marriage. In fact, I thought it was solid. He worked extremely hard and worked a lot of hours, according to him, *"for the family."* They made good money and had everything they wanted. He had been married before and had children from previous relationships, and they had children together. From the outside, they looked very happy. It seemed that everything was great. However, something he said concerned me, and it is what caused me to write this chapter. He would say, "My wife and I have the perfect marriage. Nothing could EVER happen to our marriage that would cause it to fail!"

Let's look at some positive attributes of a successful marriage. Success is different in every relationship, but certain characteristics are common in all marriages. I will list a few and then explain why success can sometimes lead to the failure of a relationship.

One aspect that makes a successful marriage is the ability for both parties to be open and honest. But it does matter how you approach each other with the truth. One author in the Bible states, "Speak the truth in love." It is imperative that each person in the relationship be able to speak his or her truth without contempt. Being able to communicate your truth allows for better communication and problem solving. I believe that one of the hindrances in a marriage is not being able to speak the truth. Many times, when one spouse attempts it, the other person creates an interruption that inhibits what is being said. The reason for an interruption is usually that there is a disagreement. When we disagree with what we hear, we use many different interruptions to cut the speaker off.

Another thing that makes a marriage successful is what John Gottman calls *partner influence.* After conducting research on husbands allowing influence from their wives, Gottman states, "Our study didn't find that men should give up all of their personal power and let their wives rule their lives. But we did find that the happiest, most stable marriages in the long run were those in which the husband did not resist sharing power and decision making with the wife." He goes on to state, "Accepting influence is an attitude, but it's also a skill that you can hone if you pay attention to how you relate to your spouse." Husband, it is okay for your wife to influence you. She has great ideas and she's smart; let her influence you. Glean from her knowledge. You don't have to know everything. In fact, you *don't* know everything, and you don't have to pretend that you do. In your personal development, it is important is to learn from others and to be influenced by those around you. Your wife can be a great influence on you.

Another aspect that brings about success in a marriage is creating a culture of grace in the home instead of suspicion or lack of trust. Creating a culture of grace in the home will allow an ease of mind in each person.

One final practice for marital success is to create face-to-face moments along with side-by-side. Side-by-side moments are the daily tasks we do with each other. They are necessities such as going to kids' sporting events, attending church services, shopping at the supermarket, participating in social activities, etc. Side-by-side tasks might change along the way, but they are the tasks that we must get done. Face-to-face time is different. These are moments when the focus is completely on just the two of you: discussing your agendas for the day before leaving for work, sitting on the couch together after a long day downloading the last few hours apart, sitting on the back porch drinking tea and talking about future hopes and dreams, going on a date while neglecting your phones except emergencies, abandoning social media while focusing on each other, and taking walks together just to talk. These are face-to-face moments that will bring about success in your marriage.

Now I will discuss two components that could cause a marriage to fail right in the middle of success.

Pride

"If it ain't broke, don't fix it!" With the couple above, both spouses were at a place where they believed nothing was broke and that nothing could ever be broke. This is where pride can sneak in and destroy the marriage. Now, I'm not referring to healthy pride, which is taking pleasure in the fact that you have a great wife or husband or children and you are proud of them. I am proud of my wife and our relationship. I am proud that she has helped me become a better person, husband, dad, and grandpa (Popie). You should develop and nurture enjoyment, joy, and pleasure in advancing in your role in the marriage as it should be—that's healthy pride. What I am referring to in this chapter is an unhealthy pride that produces arrogance and haughtiness.

Pride *can* destroy your relationship if you're not careful. Scripture informs us, "Pride goes before a fall."

You must recognize the triggers that can cause failure. You and your spouse have to be on guard at all times and not allow the picture of your marital world to be skewed by success so that you cannot see that it is in trouble. If you are not intentional and paying close attention to what is going on around you and ensuring that you are nurturing your relationship, pride will kill your marriage.

How does pride cause issues in a relationship? First, it distorts the way we interpret information that we are given. In other words, pride camouflages points of concern in issues that need to be addressed. These concerns or legitimate complaints that need to be addressed are passed off as petty matters. Pride says, "It's okay; we're good." But it's not okay. Any concern, complaint, issue, hurt, or conflict not immediately addressed will surface at some point, and usually with great intensity. The speed of a hard conversation will determine the intensity of the emotions. Pride will qualify a person as being too good to address certain issues. This will eventually backfire in a marriage.

Secondly, in a marriage, one spouse may sense that something is wrong that needs to be addressed while the other has a great deal of pride in the relationship and how great he or she thinks it is. The two are in disharmony, and one of the partners has no idea. Pride then turns to the one elevating the relationship to a point of creating a paradoxical ego. The problem is that one is drifting away while the other has no idea anything is wrong. This will continue until the one who is drifting away comes to a place where he or she has had enough or is done with the relationship and will check out. I have had couples come to my office for help just to discover that one of the parties has checked out months ago. I always ask this question when I see a couple in crisis: "Are you willing to do whatever it takes to take care of your spouse's needs without anything in return?" Many times, one will say, "I checked out weeks ago. I am just here because I told him that I would show up to the coaching session." When I hear this, my response is, "I can't help you! You are wasting your time and money." It takes both parties fully engaged to make it work. If there is just glimmer of *hope*, if both are willing, it can work. One can be full of hurt and resentment, but if they both have *hope* in their hearts for a better relationship, it can happen.

Another thing about pride that destroys the relationship is that it breeds arrogance. Nothing is more dangerous for a marriage than two spouses who are so arrogant about the solidity of their marriage that they both become blinded to *pride relationship killers.*

Pride Relationship Killers

1. Failure to admit when there is a problem

Marital problems are inevitable and have been around for at least 6,000 years. I have seen many couples who refuse to get help in their relationships because of pride. They tell themselves, "Our marriage can't be having problems." If you get anything out of this book, get this: Your marriage is no different than any other; you WILL have problems, and sometimes you will need help with a third party to help sort through them. When we are in crisis, we don't always think clearly or see things the way we need to. This is why help is so important. Your marriage is not weird. If you are having problems, you're normal. I think your marriage would be weird if you *didn't* have some sort of conflict. Your problems might be a little different from others', but you're not the only one having problems. Let someone help you.

Admitting that there is a problem will help you get back on track sooner so you can enjoy the things that make a marriage great rather than wait years in some sort of relational misery. Your relationship deserves getting back on track and moving forward. You deserve it. Your kids deserve it. Don't allow the pride of success keep you from admitting that something is wrong in your marriage.

2. Failure to listen to others around you

You know people who are nosey and are concerned more about your life and what you're doing wrong rather than about taking care of their own. However, you should have those in your circle that you trust. They are people that you have confidence in, and they sometimes see things that may be distorted to you. These people are not so close to the situation that they can't see the coming storm.

I live in Oklahoma, tornado alley. It is not uncommon to take shelter several times during the spring tornado season. Well, some take shelter. Some of us goofy Oklahomans stand out on a porch and watch the storm, even after the meteorologists have instructed us to take shelter. But it is so cool to watch those weird clouds churn, twist, and go up and down trying to develop into little tails that could possibly turn into a tornado. It's not smart, but it is a fact nonetheless.

The weatherman will say, "There is rotation in your area and a tornado is on the ground just minutes from you and headed in your direction at 30 miles per hour. It should be at your location in ten minutes; take shelter now." The radars that they use are spot on. When he gives this report, I can count on it. I can't see it, but he can, and he has tornado chasers in vehicles following the storm and reporting back to him. Even though I can't see it, he is warning me because he can see things I can't. If I fail to listen to his warnings, it could possibly be detrimental to my life and the life of my family. Why do I trust him? In the past, he has been trustworthy in his reports. He said there was a 90 percent chance of rain, and it rained. He said it would be sunny and hot; it was sunny and hot. I trust him.

It is the same way with people that you trust. Sometimes they see things that you can't. Listen to them. Listen to their warning. Not everything they say will be relevant, but at least listen, monitor, and be attentive for a while, and you will probably see what they are seeing.

3. Failure to admit the truth

There are times when problems are blatant. No one needs to say a thing. However, pride will cause us to simply not admit it. "This couldn't happen to us! Surely, this is not happening." Then, when someone asks about it, we will lie or cover it up. But I have found that over time, we can't hide it any longer. It is what it is. Admit it and fix it! I understand, no one wants to admit that one's relationship is in trouble.

I had a man come to me a few years ago who was in marital crisis. It was caused by infidelity on his part. To top it off, his career was also helping others in their marriages. He came to me for help because his wife had left him. He also wanted help from me because of my role in coaching couples. He thought the connection would fit his situation. I found out later that it was extremely difficult for him to reach out for help because he was the one who was supposed to be helping others. He had to put aside his pride if he wanted his marriage to heal. It was going to take a while for trust to be generated again by his wife, but he was desperate. Fortunately, this ended as a success story.

Apathy

Another thing that could cause a marriage to fail right in the middle of success is apathy.

The dictionary defines apathy as *a lack of interest in or concern for things that others find moving or exciting.* Apathy in this context could possibly be defined as *one becoming complacent and allowing his or her interest in or concern for the wellbeing and health of the marriage to become neglected.* I call it *unconscious awareness*, and it can be sneaky. You may not have any intentions of neglecting your mate. In fact, this could be the furthest thing from your mind. But as you get caught up in the side-by-side things of life, face-to-face moments may get neglected. You may have a tendency to get comfortable in the routine and to overlook what is needed to make the marriage work. We have a tendency to believe that things are good in our relationships and that everything will always be okay. So, we become comfortably sloppy. One could say that couples get *lazy* in their marriages.

We live in a society where it gets easy to be complacent. We want everything to be easy, and sometimes we don't want to put in too much effort into getting what we want. I know people who order a McDonald's Big Mac combo from DoorDash and pay about twice what it would cost to drive a few blocks and pick it up. Anything good in life takes work, and becoming apathetic in the relationship stems from not paying attention. In some industrial workforces, apathy on the job could possibly get someone hurt badly or even killed. Apathy in your marriage can hurt either one of you or both, maybe not in the same way as your job, but it could be tragic to your relationship.

How can we counterattack apathy? Reassess your relationship periodically, especially your role in the marriage. Are you giving the proper attention to every aspect? Are you paying close attention to the needs and desires of your mate? Do you know what he or she needs and wants? Is there something bothering you that has not been brought to your spouse's attention? Are you speaking your truth, your complaints, in love? Does he or she know that you have a problem? These are just a few questions to bring to the forefront so you can keep from becoming apathetic in your relationship. I have found that if something is continually being swept under the rug, it will always resurface, and every time it does, it will gain momentum and emotions will escalate in frustration or hurt.

Don't let success be a killer to your marriage. Nurture your success and ensure that you don't get prideful or neglectful. It is great to have a successful marriage and to hear people say to you, "Your marriage is perfect. You both are so happy, and you seem to not have any problems or arguments. How do you do it?" My wife and I get this a lot, and I can assure you that we do argue. I mess up a lot, and our marriage is not perfect. However, it looks good from the outside because we don't air our marital problems in public. We are intentional about keeping ourselves from becoming prideful. We know that we must be aware of what is going on in our marriage because something could cause it to fail if we are not attentive. Also, we stay on top of issues and problems. I feel we both have a platform to speak our truths; this will keep us from becoming apathetic.

6

Psychological Algorithm

"Developing a master-level marriage with your BFF is all about your behaviors. It is also about ensuring that concerns are communicated, and necessary tasks are completed daily to maintain a healthy marriage."
(Ronnie Gaines)

OUR LIVES ARE made up of doing step-by-step tasks throughout each day. Think about every time you cook a meal. You follow a process to get good results for your eating pleasure. Maybe you are going to bake a cake and you want it to be just right because company is coming. To accomplish this, you have to follow a step-by-step plan.

The first step is to decide what cake you want to bake and then get all of the ingredients together. Or you might prepare it right out of the box. Some of you might want to really impress your company by making it from scratch. Either way, you must follow a step-by-step plan or the cake will not come out right.

My wife is one of the greatest cooks ever, and she tried many times to encourage our daughter to join her in the kitchen to learn about cooking during her formative years. However, she just wasn't that interested. But when my daughter was about eight years old, she decided she wanted to bake a cake for the first time. My wife got out the cake mix along with all of the necessary ingredients and placed them on the cabinet for her. My wife left the room so that she could independently create this masterpiece.

A few minutes had passed. My wife hadn't heard anything except the common noises of baking a cake such as stirring, mixing, and shuffling bowls and spoons. Pretty soon my daughter yelled at her mom for help. When my wife came into the kitchen, my daughter said, "Something is wrong, Mom. This doesn't look right." My wife looked into the bowl at the cake mixture, and it was as thin as water and had no solid texture at all. It was just eggs, oil, and all the other liquid ingredients. My wife asked, "Did you put in the cake mix?" My daughter had read the instructions on the box but had missed the part about adding the contents. As soon as they emptied the box of cake mix into the bowl, it looked totally different, and the cake came out the way it was intended. And yes, we still remind her and laugh about it, even though it's now been over twenty years. It is important to follow the step-by-step plan.

In its simplest definition, an algorithm is a step-by-step procedure for solving a problem or accomplishing a task. Just like a recipe, an algorithm is following a set of instructions designed to perform a specific task. This can be a simple process such as multiplying two numbers, or it can be a complex operation such as playing a compressed video file.

When I think about an algorithm, I think of Amazon and the connection its algorithms have with social media. Have you ever been scrolling through your social media platform and suddenly you go past an advertisement about an item that you just looked up on Amazon? Creepy, isn't it? Or you "liked" something on someone else's wall on Facebook, and then you begin to see ads pop up on your wall for the very thing you just liked. Some swear by some conspiracy that our conversations can be heard by organizations through our phones. I'm not sure about that, but it is weird that I can be talking about camping and next thing I know, I am scrolling on Facebook and tent advertisements pop up.

Algorithms are set up on social media that determine the content to deliver to you based on your behavior. According to an article by Brent Barnhart on the *Sprout Social* website, "Chances are you've been recommended videos to watch on YouTube, right? This is again based on your individual behavior, digging into what you've watched in the past and what users like yourself are watching." Algorithms are all about your behavior and weeding out what is irrelevant and placing in front of you what you want.

What does this have to do with marriage? I have coined a term called *psychological algorithms*. Developing a master-level marriage with your BFF is all about your behaviors. It is also about ensuring that concerns are communicated and necessary tasks are completed daily to maintain a healthy marriage.

Tony Robbins states that there are six fundamentals that every human needs. These include certainty, uncertainty, significance, connection/love, growth, and contribution. Some of these are based on your view of your own identity and how you interact with problems, circumstances, and issues. It is how you react or how you become proactive with each one of these elements. However, in some of these categories, you have the opportunity to contribute or enhance your spouse's ability to work through them in a healthy way. In other words, if you contribute healthy behaviors with your mate continuously, they will enrich his or her life.

Again, an algorithm is a precise step-by-step plan that begins with an input and yields an output. When you create a psychological algorithm process for your marriage, it entails setting up chronological steps or protocols that will eventually lead to a desired outcome. Chronological protocols lead to triggers that yield behaviors, which bring about the necessary results. I call this process PBR (plan, behaviors, and results).

Plan

When I create a plan, I write down the process or create a journal that specifies the details. I call the process DVR (dream, vision, and reality). Dreams are just thoughts until you write them down and form a plan. When you write down your dreams, it creates vision, and then the vision can become a reality as you carry out the plan. The biblical prophet Habakkuk advised, "Write the vision and make it plain where the runner can run with it and carry out the plan." If you want to meet every need of your mate, develop a plan, write it down and make it plain, and run with it.

Any plan starts out with a problem to be solved. I'm not talking about a possible problematic relationship with your mate. You could be experiencing that, but this is more about systematic problems that every couple experiences such as communication challenges, basic neglects, or lack of love-communicating behaviors. These problems need to be addressed and solved. It's about ensuring that you demonstrate the necessary behaviors to meet the needs of your mate.

So, the *plan* begins with the end result in mind. This is where the algorithm is developed and where you find out what your spouse really needs. It's not about what you *think* he or she needs. You find this out by simply asking. One of my processes in marriage coaching is having the husband and wife write out a list of the top ten things that the other can do to demonstrate love. This is a homework assignment, and it is to be kept secret until we meet the following week. Then, I will have each person take turns and state one or two of the love-communicating behaviors until they have both exhausted their lists. This gives us the opportunity to talk through each item slowly and thoroughly. After going over the lists together, I have them give the lists to each other to refer to when creating their algorithm. I have found that using a smart phone note app is a good way to have the list with you all the time. My wife and I created our love-communicating behaviors lists sometime back. I took a picture of her list with my phone so I always have it with me.

When a plan has been created and written down as a step-by-step process, then the development of a psychological algorithm can be started by the couple. In the next part of the PBR, behaviors are implemented in the plan.

Behaviors

I have stated this before, but knowledge is not power; it is potential power. Knowledge with action is power, and a plan without action is worthless. However, a good plan coupled with action is priceless. A psychological algorithm is a step-by-step process of input that yields an output, but it is not complete without a plan and behaviors to solidify the process to acquire an outcome. They are not just certain behaviors, but they are controlled behaviors. Behaviors that are aligned with developing a psychological algorithm are actions that are a conscious competence.

For a psychological algorithm to become effective, conscious behaviors have to become intentional over time so the behaviors will become keystone habits. According to Charles Duhigg in his book, *The Power of Habit: Why We Do What We Do in Life and Business,* a keystone habit has a cue, a routine, and an outcome. In other words, the plan is the cue, the behavior is the routine, and the result is the outcome. If the process of the intentional (conscious) behaviors is continued over an extended period (competence), a healthy result will occur. If the results are not what a person wants, it's not the cue that needs to change to affect the results—it's the behaviors. If you want different results, you must change your behaviors. I often see couples who want different results in their relationships, but they continue to do the same things over and over. As we know, this is insanity!

If a couple desires different results, it takes changing habits, and the only way to change habits is to practice new behaviors. Practice doesn't make perfect; it makes permanent. If we continue to practice the wrong things or don't practice them at all, bad habits will follow and become permanent. This is a recipe for an unhealthy marriage. So the idea is to develop the right behaviors to get what you desire, and these behaviors will eventually become automatic as you practice them.

You have now created a psychological algorithm. A plan is generated, an imprint is triggered, and you automatically do it. For instance, I met with a couple recently. The husband wanted to take care of a certain task for his wife but was always forgetting. So I helped him develop a plan of triggers that would remind him to follow through with the right behaviors to get the result he wanted. One of the triggers was to set an alarm on his phone for lunch time every day. After a while, when it was time for lunch, even before the phone alarm went off, his lunch triggered the wanted response. The consistent impression of the phone alarm became such a conditioned response that soon he would not even need the alarm; it became a psychological imprint, an automatic response. Now he got the result he wanted, and she got what was needed to make her feel loved by him. The step-by-step plan and the controlled behaviors are your guideline to creating a psychological algorithm that leads to the final aspect: results.

Results

It seems that many couples want results that make a happy and healthy marriage, but they lack the tenacity to follow through with the necessary elements of the plan to make it happen. It would be nice to get results without having to go through the process of getting there. However, I have learned that the journey or the process is what truly develops character. The process of being intentional to do right takes selfishness out of our lives.

What do you want for your marriage when it comes to communication? I think everyone would say, "I just want us to communicate better." Are you willing to create a plan, write it down, and do the necessary behaviors to get your results? You may have to embrace your wife's thoughts and feelings to get the breakthrough you need. "Well, I don't always agree with her." You don't have to agree with her to hear, understand, and embrace her thoughts and feelings. Just because you hear and understand her thoughts and feelings doesn't mean that you will agree, but those thoughts and feelings are important to her. Tolerance is not agreeing with everything that your mate believes; it is sitting across from your spouse and hearing and understanding how he or she thinks and feels.

Everyone has thoughts that are not facts; they are mostly opinions. Just because I feel one way doesn't mean that it is right or wrong—it's just the way I feel. However, if I can hear and understand my wife's thoughts and feelings, even though I don't agree, it helps me have empathy for her, and I can understand why she thinks and feels the way she does. When I can fully understand her, it helps me create my step-by-step plan to carry out the necessary behaviors that will take care of *her* needs, not what I *think* she needs. When the thought of these behaviors are popping up in my head and I am following through with them, it lets her know that she is in my thoughts daily.

It is important to respond with the right actions. An algorithm process is based on the past wants of the other person. If you want your outcome to be what your spouse really wants, not so much what you want for him or her, pay close attention to what your mate likes. Just like getting a recipe right, the algorithm to please your mate must be tailored to him or her, and the end result will be that you both get your needs met.

7

Stop Getting Offended

*"Every day we have plenty of opportunities to get angry,
stressed or offended. But what you're doing when you
indulge these negative emotions is giving something
outside yourself power over your happiness."*
(Joel Osteen)

WE LIVE IN a culture in which many people are offended about everything. It is an epidemic. Someone can post on the wall of his Facebook page, and someone else will come along, read it, and post how offended he is. I realize that we may say or do things that can cause offense. However, it seems that many people are out looking for something someone said or did just so they can get offended.

I read an article recently about the 89-year-old football organization, the Washington Redskins. The Redskins organization was founded in 1932 as the Boston Braves, and after about one year, the name was changed to the Boston Redskins. The team played under this title until the organization moved to Washington in 1937. The team was originally named the Redskins to honor Native Americans in general, along with the coach and four players at that time who were Native Americans.

According to this article, the name has been a subject of debate for decades. Many believe it is a racial slur that is offensive to Native Americans. But most of those offended are not Native American. In June 2014, the U.S. Patent Office canceled the team's trademark, stating that it was "disparaging to the Native Americans." This was appealed by the owner of the organization, but in 2016 the appeal was denied by the U.S. Supreme Court. However, the U.S. Supreme Court "instead heard a similar appeal that led to a Court ruling in June 2017 that struck down the U.S. government's ban on offensive trademark registrations on First Amendment grounds." This article's headline states, "Dear white people, stop telling Native Americans like me whether we're offended by the Washington Redskins." Everyone is getting offended by something that should be offensive only to a certain group of people who are not in any way offended. People are getting offended for other people who are not offended. This is crazy!

Back in the late 1970s, there was an Eveready battery TV commercial with the famous actor Robert Conrad. The scene opened as Mr. Conrad was dressed as a boxer and was punching a speed bag. He stopped, placed a "D" size Eveready alkaline power cell battery on his shoulder, and said, "I dare you to knock this off!" I really don't understand the concept of the commercial, but it seems that our society has gotten to this point. People are walking around with batteries of offenses on their shoulders daring people, "I dare you to offend me!"

I'm sure I can find many things that I could get offended about if I search diligently enough. Almost every time, the person has no intent of offending me. So it is with our marriages. It is easy to get offended over something your wife or husband did or said. Get over yourself—not everything is about you. I have found that most of the time, my wife's words or actions that might offend me have nothing to do with me, even though they seem to be aimed at me.

My wife and I have offices that are directly across the room from each other. A few days ago, I needed to run something by her, so I went into her office. She was engrossed with something she was doing on her computer, and I walked in and immediately started asking her a question. She shot me down quickly as she said, "Hold on a second!" It seemed kind of harsh. In fact, I turned and walked out of her office and immediately started to get offended. *How dare her snap back at me like that? What I had to tell her was important.* Then it hit me suddenly: *Why are you getting offended?* I realized that I had butted in on what she was doing, and if she had allowed me to interrupt her, she would have lost her train of thought. I thought to myself, *Stop getting offended; it has nothing to do with you.* In a few minutes, after she finished the task that was consuming her thoughts, she came to my office to find out what I needed.

How often does this happen in your marriage, when one of you gets offended and it causes a major blowup in your relationship? STOP GETTING OFFENDED! Stop letting your marriage follow the pattern of our culture where you are offended about everything someone says or does. Don't let culture determine your attitude; create a culture in your marriage that says, "I will not get offended." If there are times when you try to talk with your spouse and it seems that he or she bites back at you, something else is usually wrong. An underlying problem needs to be addressed and worked out. He does not need you to be offended every time he says something in a rough tone. She does not need you to walk off in a huff and be offended every time she is a little harsh. Most of the time, you are not the problem; the problem is the problem. He or she is either working through it, is stressed by it, or is simply distracted, and it comes off as harsh or negative.

I have not always handled situations like this in a non-offensive manner, but ever since that particular moment, I've realized that it is ridiculous, selfish, and childish to get offended. I now use that teaching moment to my advantage, and I see things much differently. What would it look like in your marriage if you stop getting offended about every little thing and be reasonable and rational about every conversation instead?

How do you do this? How do you control your defense mechanism? First, realize that everyone has one. I have seen this in every couple that I have ever coached. My wife and I even have one. You don't have to let it control you. Stop taking everything personally. Stop getting defensive every time something seems harsh. Again, not everything is about you. It has everything to do with what you believe about the information you receive and how you interpret it. Let's say that your wife or husband says something to you or does something that triggers your defense mechanism. I know that this will happen at warp speed, but let's do this in slow motion.

You walk into the room and say something in general to your spouse. It sounds something like this: "Can you hold on a second? I am in the middle of something." BOOM! the defense mechanism is activated.

What you wanted to say was very important and you try to persist. "Hey, I am trying to tell you something."

"Would you just give me one minute?"

You stomp out and think, *Forget that; I'm not even going to tell you with that attitude.*

Your defense mechanism did it; it got you riled and defensive, and you let it happen. The information you received was that your spouse stopped you from saying what you were going to say. You interpreted it as what you were going to say was less important, and you gave in to the defense mechanism. Now you are offended, and you will likely be upset and sarcastic if he or she comes to you to find out what you wanted. This is a pattern in your relationship. Here goes the proverbial marital dance.

However, if you would interpret the information differently and instead walk away and continue what you were doing until your spouse is free and can give you the attention you need, it will change the trajectory of your day. This process puts you in a state of psychological relaxation rather than tension. When you are in a state of psychological tension because of a perceived offense, you will say things you wish you hadn't said, and you will remain in a defensive mood. But if you put yourself in a place of psychological rest by not getting offended, you will think more clearly and be able to reason better, and your marriage will be a quality BFF relationship.

8

Maximize Your Marriage

"Start maximizing what you have, instead of worrying about what you don't have."
(Tony Curl)

FROM 1975 TO 1991, the Gillette company experienced three separate attacks that threatened the demise of the company. These attacks, if successful, would have destroyed this amazing organization. Today, Gillette produces razors and trimmers, beard and body care products, heated razors, and antiperspirants and deodorants. They now have a Gillette Mach3 razor, which they tout as built for precision, made for comfort, with stronger-than-steel blades. Stronger than steel! That's some fancy marketing. Maybe they will soon come out with a five blade that is made of military-grade steel, whatever that means.

Two of the hostile attacks came from Revlon's leadership, which had a reputation of breaking apart companies to pay down junk bonds and to finance more hostile raids. The third attack came from an investment group that bought 5.9 percent of the company stock and attempted to seize the board, hoping to sell the company to the highest bidder and pocket some quick gains on the stock. If Gillette had flipped to this scheme, shareowners would have reaped an instantaneous 44 percent gain on their stock. Executives would have scored millions! However, Colman Mockler, then CEO of Gillette, did not cave to this idea, even though he would have profited greatly himself.

Mockler was a quiet, reserved man, and many have mistaken his nature as weak. But his goal was not to capitalize for himself, but it was to *maximize* the potential for the company for more greatness, not just for himself or other execs. He is what Jim Collins in his book, *Good to Great: Why Some Companies Make the Leap and Others Don't*, calls a Level 5 leader. He states,

> Level 5 leaders channel their ego needs away from themselves and into the larger goal of building a great company. It's not that Level 5 leaders have no ego or self-interest. Indeed, they are incredibly ambitious—but their ambition is first and foremost for the institution, not themselves.

In other words, his leadership skill was all about *maximizing* the institution over his personal ego.

Mockler didn't cave to the other voices; instead, he remained consistent in his thinking and chose to fight for the greater good of the company rather than a personal agenda. He would have profited and pocketed some great cash if he would have caved. Mockler and the other executives of Gillette staked the company's future on a large number of investments in some new technologically advanced systems, one of them being the stronger-than-steel Mach3 razor. Just think—if Mockler would have given in to the voices and let the takeover happen, the Mach3 would not exist along with other items such as Sensor and Sensor for Women, thus leaving us with a more painful shave and with the battle of the stubble.

According to Jim Collins, if Mockler would have sold out, it "would have made short-term shareflippers happy but would have been utterly irresponsible to long-term shareholders." In fact, because of the results of Mockler's decision, shareholders dodged a three-times-worse loss by just staying with Gillette. By doing what was necessary to maximize the company's health, in 2020, Gillette's net sales rose to $17.09 billion, beating the analysts' average estimate of $16.86 billion. That's a lot of stronger-than-steel blades!

In this section, I want to give you three factors that will help you *maximize* your BFF relationship. It is imperative that both of you become Level 5 leaders in your marriage. It is truly necessary, as Jim Collins states that a company builds enduring greatness through "a paradoxical blend of personal humility and professional will." You could say it like this: "Create a paradoxical blend of personal humility and the will to *maximize* your marriage, and make it everything that it needs to be to become successful."

Many voices could cause your BFF relationship to fail. Some have no agenda to destroy your marriage, but they are the opposite of what you should do to *maximize* your marriage. However, some voices, as in the example of Gillette, will attempt to alter the way you do things in your relationship, which could bring about its demise. Sometimes, those who have unhealthy marriages will want everyone else to be just as miserable. In comparison, there are some who are envious of you and your BFF, and they seem to want to tear it down so they don't feel so bad about theirs. Be like the CEO of Gillette—don't let other voices determine your marital success. Develop ways to *maximize* your marriage and thrive despite your one-star critics. Those critics should NEVER have anything to say in your life at all. Strive and thrive as you *maximize your marriage*. In the next three sections, I will give you three ways to *maximize your marriage*. Your BFF will thank you.

Revere Your Marriage

A few years ago, I sat in my office coaching a toxic married couple. They were toxic to themselves, to each other, and to me. I would always try to place them in my schedule so they were not the last couple I saw for the evening. I often see couples later in the evening because of work schedules. I always love to do premarital coaching as the last couple for the day because it is so nourishing to my soul to spend time with individuals who are happy, joyful, grateful, and pleasant. When I would head home after seeing a premarital couple, the drive would be so refreshing, and I would be in a state of psychological relaxation.

However, when I would meet with this couple, it was so toxic and in such chaos that I would leave the office in a state of psychological tension. I felt as if I had been in a wrestling match, and I was exhausted. Now you see why

I wanted their appointment to be earlier in the evening. I wanted to drive home relaxed instead of feeling as if I'd stuck my finger in a light socket. If a police officer would have stopped me on my way home after seeing them, he would think that I was a psycho or high on an illegal substance. I'm not a drinker, but there were times when I wanted to consume alcohol so it would numb me, no matter how bad it tasted. You get the picture.

I have never seen two people who would criticize and demean each other to each other's face, right in the room. I could not figure out how those two could still be living in the same house. It was horrible! They would literally scream at each other and then laugh at the other when he or she would say something extremely damaging. One time, I just let them go at it. It was a show to see. However, another therapist in the next room who was seeing a client knocked on the door and asked that we keep it down; we were interrupting other clients. Actually, I think it was aimed more at me for allowing it. The other therapist was looking at me as if to say, "Can you not contain your clients?" I got the message.

This contempt and horror went on for about an hour until I spoke up and stopped the circus. I said, "Okay, here's the deal. I have sat here and listened to you bark, bite, yell, scream, criticize, condemn, blast, and do everything in your power to hurt each other. It stops now!" I went on to say, "If you want me to see you and help you, there are some new rules. You WILL NOT speak to each other like this, in this room, anymore. You WILL NOT degrade, scream, try to hurt, show contempt, or be mean in any way to each other while you are in my presence. I will control the session, not you. You will come in, be civil, and you will treat each other as human beings, not some dog that you despise." I followed up with this: "When you walk out of here tonight, you will either schedule the next session where you will do what I say, or you can just walk out and never have to see me again. You can yell and scream at each other at home for free. You WILL NOT come here and pay me to sit and listen at you scream. Save your money."

At that point, I didn't know whether I still had them as clients or not. However, it became so quiet in the room you could hear a pin drop. I'll bet the therapist in the next office thought, *Did he kill them, or did they leave?* I said, "This session is over." Neither one of them said a word. They got up, walked out to the lobby, and scheduled an appointment for the next week.

The first thing I want you to see if you want to *maximize* your BFF relationship is to *revere your marriage*. Revere means to feel a deep respect or admiration for someone. But I see reverence as more than a feeling—it is also an *action*. It is to treat someone with deep respect. I have seen many couples treat their friends better than they treat each other. In fact, I've seen couples treat animals better. It MUST be different if you want to *maximize* your BFF relationship. She is precious! He is a treasure! Your relationship is priceless! When you understand and value who your mate really is, you will revere him or her. I want to give you two ways to revere your relationship and maximize your marriage.

Who Is Your Spouse, Really?

Your BFF is the most precious person in your life. You have been given and have chosen someone who will share in everything you have in life from here on out. You will most likely have kids who will share your DNA, personalities, likes, dislikes, beliefs, and attitudes. So watch what you do and say. You will create offspring who will be a part of the both of you. When you look at your kids, you will see a confluence of the two of you. I know that is a little scary, but it's true.

You may have a different belief from what I have, but I believe that humankind was created by God and in His likeness. The Scriptures tell us that God created the man (Adam) from the dust of the earth. Apparently, He scooped up some dirt and put together a form that was in His own likeness and called him man. I know this is difficult to imagine, but I believe it is a lot better than a sea creature swimming up to the shore and growing legs, then evolving into a monkey-like figure and then eventually looking like you and me today. I believe it would take a lot more faith to believe a story like that than to believe and hold to the fact that a God would create a man from dirt. I'll just stick to my faith in the Bible.

When God formed man with His own hands, He then breathed into his nostrils, and he became a *living* being. This was a holy and sacred formation. Then God gave the man holy anesthesia and put him to sleep and performed the first recorded surgery. He cut Adam open and took out a rib, sewed him back up, and created a woman from the rib. She was different from any other created being. The man was formed from the ground, as were the animals. The woman, however, was created from the man. She was a unique human being. The creation of the man was sacred, and when the woman was created from the rib of the man, the confluence of the two allowed a sacred union. The two became *one*. The BFF relationship is truly sacred. This is why it is so important to revere your relationship; it is a unique union created by God.

Who is your husband to you? He is in the image of his Creator. Who is your wife to you? She is a product of you, who is in the image of God. Both of you are holy and sacred. This makes the BFF relationship holy and sacred. How we treat each other is a direct reflection of how we treat God our Creator. We must view each other as sacred. We must see each other as important because God created us in His image. When you can see each other in this way, you will revere each other. You may say, "What if he is not acting very godly but more like a jack wagon?" Well, there are times when we don't act very godly. We may be created in His likeness, but we are not God. We mess up. We make mistakes. "What if she is not acting as if she's sacred?" It's going to happen, but don't lose your focus on the overall idea that the both of you are holy and sacred beings. Treat each other as such, and when you really understand who you are, you will adjust and act in ways to honor and revere each other.

Add Value to Your BFF

I want you to see that your BFF is of great value to you. Each person has his or her own strengths and weaknesses. There is no one like you. You are unique in so many ways, and you have been dealt abilities, talents, and gifts that no other person has. The psalmist states that you are fearfully and wonderfully made; you are a masterpiece. In your relationship, you bring these qualities in a way that only you can. As I've said before, you don't complete your spouse; you add to his or her life. Just as you have many strengths, you have weaknesses as well.

We all have things that we cannot do as well as others, and we don't have to. When you are weak in an area, or just not that good at it, don't waste very much time in that area. Spend most of your time developing and nurturing your strengths; spend little time in your weaknesses. I do believe that there are some things that we can get better at and we should work on those areas, but when it comes to marriage, my weaknesses are strengthened by my wife, and I come along with my wife and add strength to her weaknesses. You don't have to remind your mate of his or her weaknesses. In fact, let me say it like this: "Stop pointing out your spouse's weaknesses and affirm his or her strengths." You cannot over affirm anyone.

One of the things I see in many couples is that one spouse, most often the husband, is very limited in affirming the other's strengths. He will spend most of the time talking about his own strengths and trying to get his wife to be more like him or pointing out where she is weak. This is not how a person adds value to his or her BFF.

I have an exercise that I give to couples when they come to my office, whether for premarital or marriage coaching. I give each spouse a sheet of paper that has several adjectives that would describe an individual such as passionate, powerful, loving, generous, confident, courageous, strong, positive, and many others. I have each person circle every adjective that would describe his or her BFF. Once every defining word is circled, I have each spouse list the top five. Then I instruct each of them to affirm the characteristics every time he or she sees the other display this behavior. Make it authentic; don't just say robotically, "I like the way you do that," but say it like you mean it. "I am so thankful that you are a supporter of this family. I love how you work hard so we are taken care of." "I love how you show compassion. You are so patient and kind with our kids."

My wife and I have opposite personalities. She is an introvert, and I am an extrovert. When we go into a room full of people, she is not in her element. If it is a one-on-one meeting, she is okay, but in a crowded room, nope! However, I am energized by people. I will say, though, I sometimes love the alone time of reading, studying, or just relaxing, but I gain energy from people. When I walk into a room, I work it. There will be no strangers when I leave. Some people will dodge me, but I won't leave the room without saying something to them. Introverts hate to see me coming; they will hide from me.

Being a pastor, many times people will get upset and move on to another church. That's just the way it is. Many pastors will take this personally and do everything in their power to ignore or neglect them when they see them in public. I am not that way. In fact, when I see them in Walmart, I make it a point to go straight to them and hug them or say hi to them. I have actually had some of them see me and dart down the opposite aisle to avoid me. But I know how to do this. I see which way they are going, and I go in that direction to head them off. It is probably really awkward to them, but I'm not going to hold any grudges. I just hug them and say, "It's good to see you!" They usually say the same thing back, but I'm not sure if I buy it.

I am my wife's strength when we go into a room full of people. She will either stay behind me or will find a corner to back up to until it is time to leave. I take care of her, though. I don't ask her to be like me, nor do I demand that she be more outgoing. It is not her personality, and I'll cover for her. She knows that it is my personality to work a room full of people, so she just backs up to the corner and lets me be me.

On the flip side of that, I have a tough time being compassionate. I like people, but I have little patience. My wife, on the other hand, is very compassionate and can cry on demand. But she doesn't just cry—she is truly a compassionate person, and she has taught me to be compassionate. I am still a work in progress, but I am getting better. If you want to *maximize* and revere your marriage, add value to each other!

Work diligently on revering your marriage, even when the other person is not fully doing his or her part. It takes the both of you working together, but sometimes one of you will have a bad day. Have a hard conversation, get back on track, talk about this chapter together, and revere your BFF relationship. You were created for each other to meet each other's needs and to be everything you need to be for each other.

Let Your Mate Influence You

The couple I referred to in the last section was a good example of two people not allowing themselves to be influenced by each other; they personified the extreme opposite. For instance, if the wife tried to help her husband understand a certain situation and how she felt, believed, and perceived it, the husband would laugh, make fun of her, or put up his hand in a gesture as if to say, "Talk to the hand." I have seen this pattern in many couples. It is so disrespectful. I wonder how a husband and wife can stay together if they continue this sort of behavior. How can a couple endure so much negativity? It is toxic to the relationship. John Gottman, in just about every book he has published, states that any couple with this kind of toxicity of negative interactions will eventually divorce. It is just not possible to stay in this sort of environment.

Something that will give you and your spouse the opportunity to *maximize* your relationship is to allow yourselves to be influenced by each other. It doesn't make you the weaker person to let your mate influence you or prove that you are insufficient in the marriage. Sometimes men think that they must know everything. We have a tendency or a need to fix everything, and to accomplish this, we would need to know everything. But she doesn't want or need you to fix everything. Ladies are not inferior to the male species. I've seen a lot of capable ladies who can do so much more than some men in certain things.

God created each of us with exclusive abilities. I can do some things my wife can't, and she will ask me to help her. If you were to see me in person, it would be obvious that I am not an Arnold Schwarzenegger or a Lou Ferrigno. However, I can lift quite a lot more than my wife can, and when she needs something lifted, she will ask me to do it. When I do, she'll act as if I am all that, but I just roll my eyes and say, "Yeah, right!"

On the flip side of that, she knows and can do things that I don't know and cannot do. It is okay for you to ask your mate for advice, help, information, guidance, and even counsel. I've had occasions when I wish I had asked my wife about doing something before I did it—it could have saved me some heartache. I've also had times when I didn't let her influence me, and it backfired. Research conducted by John Gottman and his wife "showed that men who accept influence from their female partners tend to have happier and more satisfying relationships." Influencing each other displays and promotes fairness in the relationship.

I met with a couple a few years ago who wanted some marital enrichment. They were doing really well as a couple, but they felt that some things needed attention and that the best way to work through this was to see a coach or third party. There was no major crisis; they just wanted to fine-tune their relationship. I love to see couples who are doing great but want to go over the top in their marriages, those who are willing to go the extra mile to make their relationships better than ever.

Most issues were easy to adjust and work on except one: he would not let her influence him, or he didn't feel she was smart enough to do so. He was extremely sharp when it came to technology and working on car engines, among other IT-type things. She was sweet, great with their kids, smart, kind, and a great individual, and he loved her. However, she was not on the same level as he was intellectually; she did not have the same level of vocabulary as he did, and she didn't grow up in an environment of intellect as he did. This didn't make her in any way inferior, nor did it make her unwise; she was just different.

In some of the sessions, he would criticize her for not saying the correct word or the word he would use to describe something. He would correct her, and I could tell that it made her feel inferior. She even made comments that she wasn't as smart as he was. As I watched them interact, I could tell that she felt inferior to him, and he felt superior on many issues. The more I worked with them, the more I discovered that he didn't even realize he was doing this to her. Such a pattern can become a habit and can be tolerated for so long that neither of them realizes how demeaning this can be. I worked with them on letting her influence him more. This was difficult for him; he had been the "brains" of the relationship for so long that it was tough for both of them. This couple is still working on this part of their relationship. I'm not sure how it is going now, but I hope that she is able to be a voice and that he lets her influence him, even though it is not exactly how he thinks.

On the flip side of that, I have watched a couple over several years, though I've never coached them. She is the one who makes all of the decisions, controls the home, and forces her superiority over him. She has two or three college degrees and brings this to the forefront if discussing self-accolades. I'm not sure if this is the reason she is so controlling or if it is just her nature. They are in their 70s now and have been married for many years. People might say, "Leave it alone; it works for them." But what I have seen in this couple over the years is misery. If he says anything in contrast to her, she shoots him down. If he says anything that she agrees with, she dominates the conversation and makes it her idea. Many times, I have seen him look like a whipped pup. I believe after all of these years, it's easier for him to let her be the top dog and not rock the boat. How sad! What a blissful life they could have if they would each allow the other to be an influence.

My wife and I laugh at her grandparents, who are no longer alive. Her grandmother was just like the story above. Poor ol' Gramps never had any say; she was the influence in that family, and she was vocal about it. He just let her be the influence. I can remember one day we were visiting them when they were getting up in age. She rattled off something to boss him, and Gramps, with his low-toned voice, popped off something like, "You're not going to tell me what to do!" thinking that she didn't hear him.

Well, she did hear him, and she retorted, "Listen here, if you wanted to be the boss in this house, you should have started that fifty years ago. You can't start now!"

Gramps just mumbled something else under his breath, and we all just shook our heads and laughed. I am sure he was getting in the last word, but he didn't want her to hear it.

These stories are not maximized marriages. Some will live miserable lives but others will not survive. Just because you say, "Yes, dear," it does not mean everything is okay. You don't have to comply or go along with your mate for him or her to influence you. Gottman says that influencing your mate is all about being open to the ideas and opinions of your husband or wife. You don't have to agree with your spouse on everything.

One of the ways I coach couples is to let them know that they don't have to agree with everything to communicate well or to allow each other to be an influence. You don't have to give in or comply with everything for your mate to influence you. Just let your spouse know that he or she has a legitimate point of view. You can welcome a point of view without agreeing with it. Just hear, understand, and know that it is true to your mate. Maybe if you listen intently and let your spouse's idea influence you instead of shutting it out as irrelevant, you might find out it's a solid idea and you could change your perspective. You must put aside your pride and say to yourself, *This is right and I need to listen and be influenced instead of being stubborn.*

Letting your mate influence you shows that he or she is important. If you use a soft approach when you don't agree with your spouse and let her or him influence you, your mate could also see that your idea may be right instead and that what you are presenting matters. You don't always need to have your own way.

How do couples accept influence? Gottman lists four things that help couples learn to accept the influence from each other.

Check Yourself

Everything starts with you. If you're like most, you want to have a maximized marriage and truly don't want your mate to feel inferior. You most likely are not trying to keep your wife or husband from influencing you. Sometimes, individuals are so hung up on their opinions that when expressing them, they are thinking that only their viewpoints matter. Check yourself and stay open minded as you listen to the opinions of your mate and let him or her influence you. In the end, your idea or opinion may still be the right one.

Listen with Curiosity to the Other Point of View

Mutual understanding is the key to this point. Many times in our marriage, I didn't listen. I had a certain concept in my mind, and I was oblivious to any other idea or opinion. I was so set that I could not hear anything my wife was saying. One of the key features of mutual understanding is not just agreeing, but it is also hearing and understanding correctly from your mate's perspective, not yours. This can be extremely difficult when one person disagrees with what is said, but you both will come out better if the two of you will hear and understand each other clearly.

Remember the Research

Gottman talks about his research on partners who accepted influence; they tend to be happier. The more you accept your spouse's influence, the more influential you will be. The more you embrace his or her ideas, opinions, concerns, the more influential you will become.

Look for Ways to Say "Yes"

Abstain from being defensive when your mate is bidding for you to influence him or her. It is a benefit to your relationship to give in a bit, at least to see another perspective. If we stay closed minded, we could miss some great ideas. I have found that when I shoot down my wife from expressing her ideas and opinions, she tends to lock up and shut down. When she feels that she is not heard, she will disconnect.

Saying yes to your mate might be as simple as acknowledging his or her opinion, not caving to eliminate your opinion. For some, it will be extremely difficult to take a step back and embrace another idea. In contrast, for some, it may be difficult to keep from shutting down and not pursuing their ideas and opinions until they are heard and understood. However, the idea is to be in unity. Remember, unity is not the same as uniformity. Unity is accepting influence from each other and making your BFF relationship one that is blissful, not dreadful. Gottman says, "Do you want to be right, or do you want to stay together?"

Start today allowing your BFF to influence you. Make it a point in the next few days to be intentional about noticing how you act or react to your spouse's ideas and opinions. Come up with some scenarios about how your marriage usually gets in trouble in situations like these. Journal different responses that will enable you to look for ways to say yes. Listen to her intently. Hear him with an open mind. Don't rush to shoot down an idea or opinion. Even when you have clarity, use your response wisely to communicate your thoughts, ideas, and opinions without making it sound as if you have the best idea. Mutual understanding is the key, not just agreeing. Accepting influence from your BFF really does start with you making it about the two of you.

Be Present

Today we kick back in our easy chairs and with just a few touches of the remote, we can be entertained by a show that was recorded weeks ago. Not only can we enjoy the show of choice, but we also have the ability to click on a kangaroo icon that will eradicate all of those annoying commercials. I can't imagine a company these days paying millions of dollars for a thirty-second advertisement with the hope that a small percentage of viewers will actually watch the entire thing. What a tough world for companies. It takes great marketing creativity by these organizations to get people to refrain from clicking the skip button and watch for those few seconds. The fast-paced world we live in doesn't make it any easier, either. Anything we want is just a click away; no more long waiting.

I love sitting down in my recliner in the evening and watching some favorite shows. I love that we have phones that give us access to anything we need. You can shop on Amazon and choose anything you can imagine to fulfill a desire, click on the item, submit the order, and literally go to bed and get it on your door step the next day.

Technology is increasing so rapidly that just about the time you get your iCloud content moved to a new iPhone, a new one comes out. The cameras on these phones are amazing. I remember when we thought a Polaroid camera was the most amazing thing ever. Just click, wait for the picture to roll out, fan it, and presto, a halfway decent-looking photo. Or snap the picture and take the negatives to a one-hour photo shop to get good-looking photos in an hour. Today, you can take fifty pictures in five seconds on your smart phone, and within one minute delete most of them and keep just one that is Facebook worthy, and it is a quality, HD photo. Amazing!

iPhones and DVRs are great and extremely afford-able, entertaining, fun, and good tools, but they can be the most controlling, devastating, and marriage-destroying pieces of technology ever created. According to eMarketer, the average U.S. adult spends three hours and forty-three minutes per day on their mobile devices. That is just the average; many spend much more than that. Most people check their phones fifty-eight times per day. Although being on the phone almost four hours a day is crazy, the real problem is how many times a person is checking it. This means that the average person checks his or her phone seven times in one hour. What does this mean? The average American checks his or her phone, during their wake time of sixteen hours, every sixteen minutes. Every sixteen minutes, a person is distracted by his or her phone, and most of that is checking social media.

Now let's take this a little further. According to the A.C. Nielsen Co., the average American watches more than four hours of TV each day. Remember, this is an average, so almost 50 percent watch more. This breaks down to twenty-eight hours per week, two months of nonstop TV per year, or in a sixty-five-year life span, nine years glued to the tube. To add to this, a huge majority of these individuals are checking their phones every few minutes while watching TV. In other words, we live in a culture that is never really *present* anywhere.

Americans are spending eight-plus hours per day on social media and TV and still putting in eight or more hours of work. This is an indication of why relationships are failing. It would be safe to say that a lot of social media time, or TV time at that, is when the couple should be spending face-to-face time. Many couples that come to my office for coaching are having issues because at least one spouse is on his or her phone all the time, and it is causing major problems. They go out to eat to be together, and both are on their phones the entire time, not present for the moment. It is amazing to see entire families—moms, dads, and kids—on their phones in restaurants. As a society, we are missing some of the most precious moments of our lives being face-to-face as families and building memories. Instead, we are texting, surfing, and watching TikTok or YouTube videos. It is killing families.

If you want to maximize your marriage, revere it and let your mate influence you, but another major aspect is to *be present*. A few years ago, I taught a marriage series to our church. One of the nights was geared toward how to speak the truth in love by bringing up a conflict and going back and forth communicating with clarity and mutual understanding. The previous week, I picked two couples to be on stage in front of the audience as I would walk them, one couple at a time, through this process. Each couple was instructed for one of them to bring a real conflict, and I would coach them through it on stage. But they were not to talk about it prior to being on stage that night.

The wife of one couple brought up the most common conflict: cell phone issues. She stated her conflict to her husband in front of me and the audience. You could tell that this was news to him because they had not talked about it. She got somewhat emotional as she spoke her truth about him being on his phone every time they go anywhere. He paid more attention to his phone than her. He was never present with her.

When we are at work, we want to be home. When we are at home, we wish we were on the lake. When we are on the lake, we feel guilty about the yard needing to be mowed. When we are mowing, we want to be in our recliners. When we are in our recliners, we are feeling bad because we should be doing something with the kids.

When we are with the kids, we are on our phones. No one is *present* anymore.

Back to the couple above. He seemed surprised when she told him that she felt inferior to his phone. He felt bad. I think sometimes we don't really know that we are neglecting things that need attention around us. Sometimes we make excuses for being on our phones: it's work related, our parents need our attention, or friends are vying for our time. We must respond, right? My wife and I have a rule: we have our phones when we go out, but if we get a text and it is not from our kids, it can wait. Our kids know that every Friday we spend the day together; it's date day. Sometimes something will hinder this, but most every Friday, we are out, just the two of us. Okay, sometimes the grandkids are with us or we go out to eat with our kids. We love spending time with our kids and grandkids. The thing is, we don't do this all the time—Friday is our day.

This rule had to be made and enforced. We didn't always do it this way. In fact, it was because of one incident that we made the rule. I used to be that person who wasn't present, and I always had a legitimate excuse: church, people in the church, or someone really needing me. One evening, my wife and I were spending our Friday night having dinner at the Outback Steakhouse. The lights were low, music was playing in the background, a blooming onion and wheat bread were in front of us, and I was on my phone dealing with church stuff! My wife gently spoke up and said, "I guess I need to put my face on your phone so that you will look at me." Ouch! That was the wakeup call. We set the rule. We don't always do everything perfectly, but when we are together, we are *present*. I admit that sometimes we digress and find ourselves talking about the kids or grandkids, and we will laugh and say something like, "We just couldn't make it without saying something about them."

I took the couple above through a process of negotiating their cell phone dilemma. Since the two were in front of an audience, the husband wanted to be the macho man, so he said, "I will just leave my phone at home when we go out." She shook her head as if to say, *That's not the answer.* I told him that was noble of him to say that, but then I said, "You know you won't do that. Our phones are really a necessity now, and they are great in case of emergencies. You know that you won't leave it at home." So I suggested that they do the same thing that my wife and I do and make the rule of using it only if necessary.

The phone or the TV is not a bad thing unless it causes us to neglect the *present* things that are more important. If you are watching a movie, watch the movie and stay off the phone. If you are on your phone, use it and then put it down and switch to whatever else is pressing. If you are at work, be all in and do a good job for your employer; don't be miles away. If you are at an event with your kids, be present in the moment—other things can wait. And if you and your BFF are out together, be all in and create a memory of being present with each other.

If you want to maximize your marriage, revere her. Revere him. Let her influence you; she is your strength in your weakness. Let him influence you; he is your strength in your weakness. And finally, wherever you are, be present in the moment.

9

Culture of Grace

"Be generous with grace;
one day you just might need it."
(Anonymous)

IN 2015, JIM was at work as usual where he had been spending a lot of time due to the demands of his job. He was a manager of a large food chain, and the long hours, along with the stressors of pastoring a church, were overwhelming. His wife Carolyn was a great mom, a sweet human being, compassionate, understanding, and a great supportive mate for him personally and for his job. She was also an important part of the church.

One evening after work, Jim found himself in a situation with another woman who was one of his employees. This encounter would disrupt and damage their marriage. At the moment of contact, his wife, their kids, and the church flashed in his mind, but he suppressed the thoughts as he continued in the situation and then walked away with much shame and guilt. How could he face his wife? He knew he would have to confess to her because he would never be able to live with the lie that he had been unfaithful to God, her, the kids, and the congregation. He knew immediately that this would possibly be the demise of his marriage and the termination of him as pastor. How could he face his kids? How could he face his church family?

This encounter by itself, even if it had been an isolated incident, was tough, but what makes this story even more devastating is that it was the second time he had been unfaithful to Carolyn. Several years had passed since the last affair, and she had finally gotten past the hurt and had been able to trust him once again. This would for sure be the end! How could she ever make it through this? How could she possibly ever trust him again? One unfaithful moment in a marriage is devastating enough, much less two.

He followed through and walked in that night and confessed, and things unfolded just as he imagined. She was beyond devastated! Here they were years later after trust had been reestablished and now, the bottom had been busted open on the trust tub and every ounce of water (trust) flowed out. This left her completely shocked, empty, hurt, and angry, and it took her to a place of depression. He proceeded to get his things together and left home to stay with a friend, thinking that their life together was over.

You may ask, where was grace in all of this? What would you do? Just like the old adage states, "Do it to me once, shame on you. Do it to me twice, shame on me!" I would not even want to imagine what it would do to my wife if this happened to us once, much less twice. Carolyn was empty. It looked as if she had nothing left to give him.

I think we misunderstand grace. Grace is not a "get out of jail free card" every time we do something wrong so that no one can ever bring it up again. The Bible is full of grace stories. Not one story of grace in the ancient book makes it out to be something that is demanded and expected. It is offered unconditionally, but it is not cheap. According to some definitions, grace is unmerited and undeserved kindness and favor. You may say that this is Jesus' role, not mine. I think that Jesus should be a great example for us, but there are times when we may not have any more room for grace for certain people and situations. Grace is not a free-to-do-whatever-we-want card. Grace empowers us to make a change.

There is a story in the Bible about a lady who had been caught in the act of adultery. She was thrown into the middle of the street so the religious leaders could perform a public execution by stoning her to death to fulfill the law. I have a few issues with this story. First, if she was caught in the act, at least one of those men must have been following her and peeping through a window. How long did they watch before grabbing her? I want to think the men watched through the window, got their jollies, and then went in and grabbed her. Some of them could have been jealous because she wasn't with them. Second, where was the man? If she was caught in the act, the man was surely in the sack with her when they busted her. Who was he? Apparently, they let him go and focused on her as the problem.

They threw her down and picked up some stones, and then Jesus stepped in. But He did not condone her act. Jesus never tried to sweep the facts under the rug and hide that she had disobeyed the law. He exposed the act just as the religious leaders exposed it. What she did was not right. Grace does not sweep wrong things under a rug; grace exposes and empowers a person to make a change. Listen to this in a different way: *Grace does not justify; grace promotes change.* Grace is not about giving a person a wink and a nod with a free pass. Like the old saying goes, "A wink is as good as a nod to a blind mule."

When Jim breached the fidelity of his marriage, for Carolyn to offer grace was not to give the situation a wink and a nod and act as if nothing ever happened. Some might say, "The Christian thing to do would be to forgive and forget and move on, and to be thankful that he confessed." His confession was essential, but for Carolyn to forgive, forget, and trust became a long, hard journey.

As I have mentioned in another chapter, forgiveness could happen much faster than trusting again, but even forgiveness, especially in this case, could take a while. The idea is for the offender to do the right things over an extended period, which would bring about forgiveness. Then the person must begin a process of building trust. This also takes a while. Forgiveness can be a two-way street, while trust is one way. The offender must complete trustworthy interactions to gain the trust from the other party, and this takes time.

Right after Jim had this affair, Carolyn began to seek therapy to help manage everything she was experiencing. She went every week to find strength for her life and to be able to cope—not only with the offense that she had experienced, but also with the fact that her marriage could possibly be over and that her BFF had betrayed her. This process went on for several months.

In the meantime, it had been suggested to Jim that he get counseling. This is where I met Jim for the first time. He came into my office, and his narrative began. As he told me his story, I sat and listened intently for several weeks before we started the healing process. In my mind, I was thinking, *This will probably not end well.* After I heard his entire back story, the work began. We worked for several weeks, and weeks turned into months. After a while, when I realized that there was hope for recovery, the idea was to get both spouses into a sessions together. Finally, the three of us met. She sat on one end of the couch and he sat on the other. You could cut the tension with a knife.

Carolyn is a mild-mannered individual. She is soft spoken and such a sweet, kind person. However, over the next several weeks, I saw a tenacious, spirited woman who was not backing down from what needed to take place for the relationship to heal. In fact, at one point, I didn't think Jim would survive the demands made by Carolyn. These demands were fashioned in a way that he would prove his fidelity so the act of unfaithfulness would never happen again. If he did not complete this list of what she called the Ten Commandments, it was over for sure. Actually, during the onset of these sessions, she never gave any indication that the relationship would survive at all, but if he didn't complete these demands, there wouldn't be any chance of her letting him come back. Remember, grace isn't being weak and justifying; grace empowers a person to change.

Back to the story of Jesus and the woman. Jesus put the accusers on the spot, and they dropped the stones and walked away. I want to think that Jesus pointed out some of their sins and that He had every right to stone them. Or maybe, since He wrote something in the dirt, it may have been something like, "Do you want me to bring up some of the things you have been doing?" They turned and moved out of the scene quickly. But then Jesus turned to the women and said, "I don't condemn you!" He offered *grace* first. However, He didn't just leave it there; He was all about the Ten Commandments. He said, "Don't do this ever again, because it's not right." Yes, I am paraphrasing. This was all about the law. Grace doesn't make our wrong action into something that's okay. It's not okay to do things like this. It hurts people. Grace requires change while loving through it.

After several weeks of meeting with Jim and Carolyn, he worked diligently to help heal the relationship. He fulfilled every one of her Ten Commandments, and soon they were sitting on the couch hand in hand, smiling at each other and in love all over again. At one point, we brought in the kids and did a family session. I encountered grace coming out of Carolyn and the kids in a way that I have never experienced before. The time came for Jim to move back home. A few months later, he contacted me and asked if I would attend the renewal of their vows to celebrate their twenty-fifth anniversary. Of course, I would attend. I had the great privilege of praying over them during the ceremony. Today, they are happy, they are successful in business, and they have a new grandbaby. I watch her look at him and smile with great love and compassion. Now, that's grace!

I wrote this story to give you an idea of what a culture of grace looks like in a challenging situation, but I want to shift just a little and show you another view of grace in the home. Sometimes we may view a culture of grace much like the story above and how people have offered this grace in bad situations, but what about everyday life? What about just living out life face-to-face and side-by-side? I have heard it said, "Be generous with grace; one day you just might need it." What I want to communicate to you in this chapter is to create a culture of grace in the home rather than suspicion or lack of trust. Offer grace first.

It may sound something like this: "Where have you been? I have been texting you for hours and you never responded! I'll bet you did that on purpose!" *Suspicion!* "Let me see your phone; you have been texting other people but can't text me?" *Lack of trust!* Let me make something completely clear: If these things are happening habitually, it's not about grace anymore. It has now become a conflict.

A culture of grace is not just thinking about offering kindness or mercy; it extends beyond what you are thinking at the moment. I want to show you three methods of displaying grace.

Grace Sees with a New Perspective

How many times have you gotten upset over something that you thought your spouse did and you went off on them, only to find out you were wrong? Grace examines everything about the situation instead of forcing an opinion when you don't have all of the facts. Grace helps the person make a rational, cognitive appraisal and then seeks out the information necessary to understand the reason for a particular behavior. Remember from the "Change the Way You Think" chapter, our interpretation of information determines our feelings and our behaviors, which in turn will determine the effects/consequences (the outcome).

The wife is going to have dinner on the table and ready to eat when her husband gets home at 7:00, and he knows that she will be prompt. It is now 7:20, and he is not home yet. The first thought that comes to her mind is *He does not care or appreciate that I have busted my tail getting this dinner ready and on the table by 7:00. Doesn't he realize that I have worked hard today as well? He is so inconsiderate. Now it is getting cold.* What do you think his response will be if he walks in and this is what he hears? I will guarantee that he will be defensive. He will feel attacked, and any time someone feels attacked, the "fight or flight" hormone skyrockets. It may look and sound a little different in your mind and in your world, but for the most part, this is often very close to the way it plays out and the way we respond. The first thing that our minds tend to do is suspect.

Here is where it matters the most. We can either lead with the lack of trust or offer grace. This is why it is extremely important to develop a culture of grace. When we create a culture of grace ahead of time, it will be the first response rather than the alternate. If suspicion or lack of trust is the reflex, when he comes through the door at 7:20, it might sound something like what follows. Remember, she has no idea why he is late at this point.

When he walks through the door twenty minutes after dinner has been set, she goes off on him. "I have been texting you, and you have not responded at all. Where have you been? I'll bet you did all of your stuff and did not think one time about me having dinner ready! You don't even care!" He hasn't even had a chance to offer any excuse. I can tell you this—the evening will not go well.

But what if she offers grace first? Yes, dinner is cold. Yes, she has worked very hard to have it ready by 7:00. Yes, it is frustrating. However, what would it look like if grace was the automatic response rather than suspicion or lack of trust? Here is what this would look like.

She meets him at the door and says, "I am so glad you are home. I was starting to worry when I texted you several times and you didn't respond. Is everything okay?" This will change the entire evening! So she finds out that right before he walked out of the office, his boss caught him and wanted to go over some last-minute details for the next day. When he finally got into his car to leave, he still had plenty of time to make it by 7:00, but he got caught up in traffic where he had to go at a slow pace for several minutes. There was no way he could call her to let her know he was going to be late because the battery had died on his phone. He knew that when he walked through the door, she would pounce on him and chew him out. But to his surprise, when he walked in, she offered grace first. By offering grace first, it allowed her to hear and understand what actually happened. He was not being inconsiderate. It was the circumstances that caused the problem.

Think about this. If it were you running late and something held you up, you would want grace because of the circumstances: it was traffic, work, my boss, my phone, someone else's fault, etc. However, many times we want grace when it's for us, but we have a difficult time offering grace to someone else. Offer grace first; the time will come when you will need it!

Grace Resists the Urge to Focus on Faults

Can you think of five adjectives that describe your BFF's strengths? Maybe your spouse is compassionate, generous, dependable, considerate, talented, or loving. What about weaknesses? You could probably come up with two pages of those, right? I know my wife could. It's easy to focus on and come up with several weaknesses. You don't have to tell your mate his or her weaknesses; your spouse knows them by name. But strong and healthy marriages develop a culture of affirmations. You cannot affirm someone too much. Affirmations focus on the strengths of a person, not weaknesses.

Giving an affirmation is like planting a seed. If you plant affirmations often and tend and nurture them, you will create a culture of growth and harvest a life of fun, joy, and health in your marriage. You will produce some future phenomenal possibilities for your relationship. Try it right now. Pause for a moment and write down as many positive qualities as you can of your mate. Now, take the top five and begin affirming your BFF every time you see those characteristics expressed. Change your list often to affirm your spouse in all of his or her qualities.

Grace Forgives

As I have stated before, there is a difference between trust and forgiveness. Forgiveness can happen much sooner than trust. I would like to use the metaphor of a bathtub and water. I was introduced to this by my supervisor at the counseling center where I interned while earning my degree in marital and family therapy. The bathtub represents the marriage, and the water symbolizes trust. When a couple is dating and then becomes newlyweds, normally the bathtub is full of water; the spouses have full trust in each other. Of course, there may be times when he flirts a little with someone else, but he just gets an elbow in the arm and a raised eyebrow, but for the most part, no trust is lost. She could even look at another good-looking guy while they are married, but an innocent look doesn't cause any trust issues.

Now, he may have a conversation on Facebook with an old high school girlfriend and get a little too flirtatious. His wife finds the chat and pulls the plug and some water leaks out, but he apologizes, and the plug gets put back in and the leak is fixed with very little trust lost. Then something happens as in the story at the beginning of this chapter. Not only is there a leak, but there is also a hole busted in the bottom of the tub and all of the water (trust) is gone. The only way to get the trust back is to repair the hole and then begin filling the tub back up. In this situation, you cannot just throw a hose in and start filling it up; it takes time. In fact, it's like a teaspoon at a time, and each teaspoon is a trustworthy interaction. Trustworthy interactions may include giving her access to all posts and chats on Facebook and all phone calls and texts, and that she knows his exact location every minute of the day. These sorts of activities allow a spoonful of trust at a time to be added and to bring the level back up until the tub is once again full. This takes intentionality and time. This is the process for trust; however, forgiveness could come about much more quickly. Grace forgives.

I have seen some individuals who have been hurt to the point of never gaining enough trust to continue the relationship. However, over a period of time and with much grace, they were able to forgive. The relationship failed, but grace helped them forgive. The great thing about grace is that if you can ever find it in your heart to acquire a level of grace, forgiveness will happen. Grace inhibits bitterness, spite, the silent treatment, and revenge. If you will create a culture of grace in your home, it will change the life and the health of your marriage.

10

Final Thoughts

WHEN I FIRST realized that couples were falling apart even though I was teaching them many techniques and approaches, I had to make a change in what I was doing. As I discovered that it was a friendship issue, I searched for books that dealt with friendship but found very few. There are friendship books that skim the surface of being a friend, but nothing that really stood out about married couples rediscovering friendship or strengthening a BFF relationship. There wasn't anything on ways to nurture and grow the friendship with your mate.

After meeting with many couples who were experiencing this frustration, I knew a resource was needed that addressed this very thing. This is why *BFF: Becoming Your Spouse's Best Friend Again* idea was written, and it has been a breakthrough in the way I work with couples and the way that my wife and I build our marriage.

I hope this book has inspired you to re-create your marriage and rediscover your BFF. I would love to hear stories of how this book has helped you and your mate bring your marriage back to the way it started and the way it should be for the rest of your life. Please send me your stories. I would love to share with you and your BFF your best life. You can email me at info@master-levelmarriage.com.

I believe that if you follow these principles in this book, you will have a success story of your own. When you finish, go back and read it again. I believe that you will discover ideas that you might have missed the first time through. Also, when you are done, give it to another couple that you know and love. If you do not want to part with your book, purchase another copy and give it as a gift. I can't think of a better gift to give a couple whom you love—the gift of a healthy marriage. What a wedding gift.

I want to leave you with this thought. You can have a great marriage. You can become BFFs all over again. Take your marriage back to the place where you use to adore and cherish each other and wanted to be in his or her presence 24/7. Restore your relationship to the place it was intended to be. When you do this, you can be your best self, live out your full potential, and experience your best marriage with your BFF.

Appendix

Love Communicating Behaviors

Each participant will list 10 *Love Communicating Behaviors*. If their spouse did these things, he/she would feel love.

NOTE: It must be something that your spouse can do and is not a daily task (i.e. vacuum, fold clothes, clean the house, etc.).

EXAMPLES: Leave an *"I love you"* post-it-note on the bathroom mirror; send an out-of-the-blue *"love"* text in the middle of the day; drop by her place of work and take her a cup of coffee; and while she is in the shower, put a towel in the dryer and bring the warm towel to her as she gets out; etc.

1. _____

2. _____

3. _____
4. _____
5. _____
6. _____
7. _____
8. _____
9. _____
10. _____

About the Author

DR. RONNIE GAINES holds a doctor of ministry with a concentration in pastoral care and counseling and a master's in marital and family therapy. He has been involved in ministry for over thirty years as either a staff pastor, church planter, or lead pastor. Currently, he and his wife Mylisa serve as the founding and lead pastors of Extreme Church in Pryor, Oklahoma. In addition to his pastoral ministry experience, he is an assistant professor in practical ministries at Oral Roberts University in Tulsa, Oklahoma.

Dr. Gaines has a passion to assist couples in marital enrichment and to help restore marital relationships in crisis. He brings a wealth of knowledge and experience to his compassionate coaching approach to marital enrichment. He is a conference speaker and has taken his marital content internationally.

Dr. Gaines is a United States Marine Corps veteran. He and Mylisa have been married for thirty-three years and reside in Pryor, Oklahoma. They have two children, both of whom are married, and three grandsons.

Dr. Gaines has a seven-module video series and workbook titled *Transform Your Marriage in 7 Days.* You can find this on his website at www.masterlevelmarriage.com.

For more information, contact Dr. Gaines at info@ masterlevelmarriage.com.

You can also find him on Facebook at facebook.com/ drronniegaines and on Instagram at instagram.com/ drronniegaines.

CPSIA information can be obtained
at www.ICGtesting.com
Printed in the USA
FSHW020421100222
88199FS